C000071639

UNLOCK THE PSYCHIC POWERS OF YOUR UNCONSCIOUS MIND

And break free from the shackles of the old you

ANTHONY TALMAGE

UNLOCK THE PSYCHIC POWERS OF YOUR UNCONSCIOUS MIND

All rights reserved. A proportion of all royalties from sales will be donated to the Red Cross to assist with their work in various war-torn parts of the world.

Copyright © 2020 Anthony Talmage

The Mind | - the element of a person that enables them to be aware of the world and their experiences, to think, and to feel; the faculty of consciousness and thought

The left brain | - the left-hand side of the human brain, which is believed to be associated with linear and analytical thought

The right brain | - the right-hand side of the human brain, which is believed to be associated with creative thought and the emotions

The Collective Unconscious | - (in Jungian psychology) the part of the Unconscious Mind which is derived from ancestral memory and experience and is common to all humankind, as distinct from the individual's unconscious

The Infinite Mind | - a higher form of consciousness than that possessed by the ordinary person....The Unified Field that connects all Mind and matter. Everything is energy and is interconnected

Intent | - the determination to do, or achieve, something

Belief | - an acceptance that something exists or is true, especially one without proof. Trust, faith, or confidence in someone or something.

TABLE OF CONTENTS

FOREWORD

This book is the third in a series celebrating the ability of the human Mind to transcend the restrictions imposed by conventional science. My first two books *Dowse Your Way To Psychic Power* and *In Tune With The Infinite Mind* explore ways in which ordinary people can become extraordinary people. *Unlock The Psychic Powers Of Your Unconscious Mind* looks at how each of us has within us the tools to achieve the magical and miraculous. Each of us is unique and each of us is needed by the Universe to fulfil a special mission. We live in a wonderful world, full of mysteries. My aim with this book is to highlight some of those mysteries and encourage you to help unravel them and convince you why you are so important to the future of the planet.

PREFACE

In my book *In Tune With The Infinite Mind* I give concrete examples of how the human Mind has a power beyond our understanding. For instance, Western medics on a visit to a 'medicine-less' hospital in Beijing watched in amazement as, within minutes, a malignant tumour dissolved before their eyes. The local doctors explained that they didn't judge the cancer good or bad – it was just a 'quantum probability' of which there were many. They used their Minds to access the realm in which all probabilities exist simultaneously to make a different choice.

This surely supports the contention that we are not the playthings of Destiny but, in fact, we each have the power not only to change our own lives for the good but also other people's and, perhaps, even the world.

In a society in which Dark Forces seem to be gathering strength, it's understandable that we look on in despair wondering what anyone could do to halt humanity's headlong dash to destruction. How can little old me do anything to stop wars, terrorism, hatred, injustice, fear? The answer is: a lot - by tuning into the quantum universe of infinite probabilities and selecting a different outcome. We live in a holographic universe and are inter-connected with everything - to the end of eternity. Our every thought reverberates around the cosmos, affecting it for ever.

What I hope this book will prove to you is that the Universe is energy and thought is energy and that our Minds are engaged in an eternal struggle with energetic forces. But we – you - can prevail. By taking up the challenge of harnessing all potentials, you could precipitate a consciousness explosion and nudge the world towards its next evolutionary step and a better place.

There are many counter-intuitive ideas ahead. Ones with which, dear Reader, you might wish to argue. If we were sharing a glass of wine or cup of coffee we could happily debate the theories until the early hours. As we cannot, I have taken it upon myself to anticipate the cut and thrust of your passionate views in the form of a Q&A format. So, after some chapters you will assail me with your adversarial skills and even start to make me wonder. Good for you – no-one has the monopoly on truth.

**If you can change your mind, you can change your life –
William James**

1 MIND MAGIC AND MIRACLES

Consultant Dr B has a challenging list of medical cases. Timmy, aged 16, has diabetes. James is not diabetic and is a healthy six-year-old, except he can't drink orange juice without coming out in hives. Jess, aged 8, has no allergies so orange juice is not a problem but she has what ophthalmologists call a 'lazy eye' which turns inwards towards the nose. Sadly Robert, aged 19, is the only one of Dr B's patients who has a life-threatening illness. He has been diagnosed with cancer.

So, you are wondering, what's so unusual about this collection of routine medical cases? Nothing at all were it not for the fact that Timmy, James, Jess and Robert are all the same person. They are all distinct personalities who inhabit the same body. And it is a dramatic illustration of the power of the Mind which seems to have the ability to 'cure' each personality of its separate afflictions as soon as it switches to its alter-ego.

Timmy does not have diabetes when he becomes James. James can happily drink orange juice without ill-effect when he becomes Jess. Jess loses her lazy eye when adopting the personality of Robert. And, amazingly, Robert's cancer disappears when he becomes any of the others.

The phenomenon of several personalities in one body used to be known as Multiple Personality Disorder but today it's called Dissociative Identity Disorder. The medical profession treats sufferers with different protocols but rarely, if ever, stops to wonder HOW these physical changes happen as their patients swop personalities. To be honest, they probably have enough of a challenge without concerning themselves with a phenomenon which seems to involve the physical manipulation of matter with implications that are profound.

It seems that one Mind can change the physical structure of each personalities' bodies. How? How can Robert's cancer be healed in moments? Or Timmy's diabetes disappear? We'll look in more detail later at what the answers might be. But for now I hope you're beginning to see the miracle worker that you have in your head. Actually, that's not entirely true.

What you have under your skull is your brain. Your Mind is something different, but inherently bound up with your brain. Without getting into unnecessary complications at this stage let's for the time being regard both as the same thing. We'll differentiate between them when necessary.

That dichotomy is just one complication in our quest to befriend our miraculous Mind and we've hardly started! Before the end of this book I hope you will be convinced of how important you and your Mind are. And I'm not just saying this. My studies have shown me how crucial each individual person is to life, the Universe and everything. You may think that in your humdrum, daily routine you're just a faceless cog in a machine and wouldn't be missed if you just simply disappeared.

How very wrong you would be. What you say and do today can, literally, change the world. Remember the butterfly effect? The theory that a small event can cause a big change – a butterfly flaps its wings in Chicago and a tornado happens in Tokyo. And how much more powerful are you than a butterfly? And your Mind is at the heart (forgive the pun) of this proposition.

Back to the Mind. It can make magic. It can perform miracles. It can change the world. In the following pages we're going to explore together just how. We're not going to wallow in airy-fairy theories. We're going to explore the practicalities. And I might as well get a warning out of the way now before we go any further. If you're going to get the full benefit of that miracle-worker in your head you're going to have to plough through some challenging stuff. But please stick with it as, gradually, the picture will unfold and you'll learn not only how important you are to this world but how to maximise your power in it. OK, let's do it...

When you make a choice, you change the future - Deepak Chopra

2 OOPS! I'VE CREATED ANOTHER UNIVERSE

During my researches into the human Mind an important piece of the jigsaw dropped into place when I encountered the work of physicist John Archibald Wheeler. I learned we are not random individuals blundering through life trying to make the best of things. Rather we are co-creators on whom, no less, the future of the Universe depends.

While Wheeler may not be a household name, in terms of legacy he's up there with the quantum physics greats like Max Planck, Niels Bohr, Werner Heisenberg, Richard Feynman and even Albert Einstein.

Wheeler, who died in 2008 at the age of 96, was an American theoretical physicist who coined the terms 'black hole' and 'wormhole.' Another of his pithy dictums about tricky physics was his comment on Einstein's theory of relativity: 'Space-time tells matter how to move; matter tells space-time how to curve.' He gave us a clue about the power of our Minds when he explained his Anthropic Principle to an audience of fellow boffins. He said, 'The Big Bang happened because I thought of it and I thought of it because the Big Bang happened.'

His point was that human consciousness can bridge time and space. And if, according to quantum theory, the observer creates reality then we, as observers, have been a necessary part of bringing the Universe into being. We are co-creators together with an all-powerful force – call it God, the Infinite Mind, the Divine or Super intelligence, or whatever you like – which has set a limit to its own powers by decreeing that it can only create Life, the Universe and Everything by working with the consciousness of the humans it has created. So now do you get why you, a unique human being, are so crucial to unfolding events?

I believe the exciting thing is that the 'Infinite Mind' has selected each one of us to be a co-creator with a specific role – whether it is to say a kind word to a stranger or be the father of $E=MC^2$. Wheeler contended that the Universe is a work in progress and without human consciousness creation ceases.

Being an intelligent person you're not going to take my word for it, or even that of a distinguished scientist. So let's have a look at how the idea that our consciousness can affect the real world came into being. How the term, coined by pioneer experimenters, 'The Observer Creates Reality' came into general acceptance by the best scientific brains in the world. Ancient cultures have believed for millennia that humans can influence events. But boffins are a hard-nosed lot. They scoff at these primitive beliefs. At least they did until, that is, a famous breakthrough called The Double-Slit Experiment.

It was designed to settle, once and for all, the argument over whether light was made of waves or particles. If your eyes are starting to glaze over at this point, make yourself a coffee. I did warn you that it might need a bit of discipline to stick with it. I promise you it'll be worth it.

"Look here,' you might be thinking at this point, 'what the heck has waves and particles got to do with me, my Mind and how I fit into life on this planet?' Well, as I said, stick with it as we've got to lay down some foundations before we can start to build a picture. You need to know that the difference between waves and particles is actually quite profound and relevant to all that follows.

Waves are invisible vibrations and mass-less - think radio waves: you can't see them or feel them but switch on your audio system and there they are. Meanwhile, particles are tiny pieces of matter (think miniature marbles). Or things. The Double-Slit Experiment changed everything and proved to the, Oh so reluctant boffins, that 'things' were reacting to human thought. Yes, they discovered your Mind has the ability to alter reality.

According to the aforementioned physics colossus, Richard Feynman, The Double-Slit Experiment captures the central mystery of Quantum Theory. It was first carried out by Thomas Young back in 1803, but since then variations on the same theme have propelled us further and further into a real life Alice in Wonderland realm. It's almost as if we humans live in two parallel universes with different rules that overlap at the edges.

I give a full explanation of this profound experiment in my book *In Tune With The Infinite Mind* but if you haven't read it I include a summary as an appendix at the end of this book. But to summarise here: much to the frizzy-haired scientists surprise it proved that light was not just waves as previously thought, but BOTH waves and particles. However, before they could all start slapping each other on the back anticipating a Nobel Prize, they were shocked to the core at an accidental discovery during the experiment.

They found that the act of measuring what was going on actually changed the results! Somehow, human consciousness seemed to be affecting the experiments themselves. The particles, in this case photons, were reacting to the *thoughts* of the experimenters. If the scientists watched which slit the photons were going through, expecting them to create a black line on a screen the other side of the slit, they obediently did. Think of bullets being fired through a narrow opening – eventually you get a line of bullet holes matching the shape of the slit.

But, when the experimenters looked away, the particles ran riot, turned themselves into waves and made a different kind of pattern – not one line but a series, like a bar code. Look back, and the photons behave perfectly making a neat line, look away and chaos ensues with lines everywhere.

These bar code lines are known as an 'interference pattern' which is what you get when waves go through two slits – the peaks and troughs of each set of waves 'interfere' with each other and create the bar code. But watch them in action and they create just one line. As if this weird behaviour by those pesky particles wasn't enough to make the scientists want to lie down in a darkened room, further experiments revealed that the particles seemed to be able to anticipate events.

When the scientists decided to 'trick' the photons by measuring (watching) which slit they went through AFTER they had made their decision and had arrived at the other side of the opening, it made no difference. It was as if each photon knew they were going to be observed. They appeared to know exactly when the mice would be away and the cats could play, so to speak. Or when teacher would have her stern gaze on the class and they had to sit to attention and do as they were told. No amount of jiggery-pokery by the experimenters could catch them out.

After much trial, error and deliberation the scientists came to the reluctant conclusion that it was their own Minds that were forcing the particles to change their behaviour. Thus their profound conclusion that 'The Observer Creates Reality.'

Meanwhile, back in the real world that you and I live in, we don't do experiments; we just get on with our day-to-day routines but, nevertheless, we are affecting everything around us, changing the planet with our consciousness. Things will get a bit clearer if we move on to the next level where our acts of creation are being caused by what particle physicists call the 'collapse of the wave function.' This description is typical boffin-babble, designed to confuse us lesser mortals. All it means is that our Minds have brought into being a particular outcome from an infinite number of probabilities.

To put it simply, quantum theory says that a quantum particle doesn't exist in one state or another, but in all possible states all at the same time. It's only when we 'observe' its state that a quantum particle is essentially forced to choose one form of existence, and that's the state that we bring into being. You think about it and its 'wave function' (infinite probabilities) collapses and we conjure a single new reality (remember the tumour in the medicine-less hospital?).

It's as though reality is an unset jelly. Our act of observation causes the jelly to set and a new reality is born. If you're still a bit confused about this quantum stuff, how I look at it might help you get your head round its weird concept. For centuries humankind was happy to go along with scientists' views that the Universe was what they called 'deterministic.' Everything functioned like a well-oiled clock; it was mechanical, predictable and obvious. If you rolled one billiard ball against another, the force would ping them into new directions.

On a bigger scale, the sun would come up and go down in a predictable cycle, the planets would whirl about it in a way you could set your clock by and everything in the garden was lovely. Until those pesky scientists went and upset the applecart by discovering the microscopic world inside an atom.

Why, we all might ask, does it matter how particles and their even smaller components – quarks - behave? It does, simply because everything in the Universe is made from them. So while the sun comfortingly keeps our planet safe with its predictable routine, its atoms and particles break every rule physicists ever conceived. Look at it this way: a coin has two sides – heads and tails. When you spin a coin, one side or the other comes down. You can flick it a million times and a million times it will either be heads or tails.

But, in the quantum world the coin could come down both heads and tails at the same time! And it can come down in front of you - and in the next room. Or in the next universe. In quantum-speak it's in a 'superposition' – all possibilities at the same time. But, once the human 'observes' the process just one possibility is conjured into being. By the way, don't get hung up on the word 'observe.' What we mean is an *intentional* engagement by human consciousness. For our purposes, deliberately thinking about something is as good as 'observing.'

Even though this seemingly-impossible discovery – 'The Observer Creates Reality' - happened 100 years ago, a large proportion of scientists today still agree with the proposition. Father of the theory was Danish physicist Niels Bohr and it became known at the Copenhagen Interpretation – that the act of observing a sub-atomic particle forces it to 'choose' how it's going to manifest itself out of billions of states. This became the orthodox view of quantum mechanics.

So, whether they liked it or not (and many of them did not like it one bit) the brain boxes had to admit that the human Mind brings things into being left, right and centre. Fast forward to today and, while many still adhere to the Copenhagen Interpretation, a different theory is beginning to give it a run for its money. One reason is that it removes many of the seeming paradoxes of Copenhagen. This controversial new interpretation was invented by American physicist Hugh Everett, a pupil of our friend John Wheeler.

Everett came up with it in 1957 and it became known as the 'Many Worlds Theory.' This does away with the observer creating reality and collapsing wave functions. Instead, Everett reckoned that each time we humans make a binary choice – Shall I go to the supermarket or take the dog for a walk? – We create alternative universes in which one of us does the weekly shop and the other self trots off with Fido.

We only see one of those realities, but the other has a separate physical existence too, says Everett. According to him we don't 'create' reality we merely 'select' one from the infinite number on offer. And the other one in our Minds which we don't select takes on a life of its own. Crazy or what? This is just one aspect of the Alice in Wonderland realm the quantum world is.   But, whether it's the Copenhagen Interpretation or the Many Worlds Theory, either way our Minds call the shots and new realities come into being as a result.

As Wheeler said, 'I think we are beginning to suspect that man is not a tiny cog that doesn't really make much difference to the running of the huge machine, but rather that there is a much more intimate tie between man and the Universe than we heretofore suspected.' He also said, 'The Universe does not exist "out there," independent of us. We are inescapably involved in bringing about that which appears to be happening.   We are not only observers.   We are participators.   In some strange sense, this is a participatory universe.'

All this sounds very grand and counter-intuitive. How could we, mere humble humans, be creating universes with our Minds? How can our Minds change the molecular structure of human bodies? How can we possibly create THINGS? At this point it may be worth remembering that scientists all agree that solid matter is made of atoms and that atoms are 99.99% empty space! The chair you're sitting on, the book you're holding, the home you're living in are all mostly empty space. They are all *energy*.

Einstein said, ' Everything is energy and energy is everything.' And our intentions affect the energy around us. The trick to creating matter is to organise the energy and it's our Minds that do the organising. The German theoretical physicist and Nobel laureate Max Planck, said, 'I regard matter as a derivative of consciousness.' Or putting it another way, the human Mind is a catalyst that brings into being a reality which is already there in the cosmic field.

The manifestations of the quantum world are out of this world. Those of us for whom the quantum realm is the stuff of frizzy-haired geniuses can take heart. Frizzy-haired geniuses don't know what's going on either. But something remarkable is happening, the greater understanding of which could change human destiny. And you are part of it.

OK, this seems a good time to pause for any questions you might have. By the way, to keep the format as simple as possible, your questions are in bold and my answers are in plain text.

You were right, it is a bit heavy going. I bought this book because I'm interested in how I can better use the talents I've got and live a more productive life and I'm not sure where this quantum stuff comes in. I know it's probably exciting to people who understand the science but I'm looking for something that deals with real life.

It does deal with real life and we're getting there. But wading through these quantum thickets are necessary and that's why I included a warning early on. Even the basics of Quantum Theory can seem hard going and irrelevant to most people. But please stick with it as it is relevant and there's lots of real life material ahead which will make more sense if you can view it with some knowledge of the Quantum world.

Fair enough. I confess I had a sneaky look at the next chapter and it does look intriguing.

Whoever is strong in mind and spirit will have power over them - Fyodor Dostoevsky

3 NOW WE'VE MADE A GHOST – AND IT'S CHASING US

So far we've looked at the Mind's ability, internally, to programme the body's trillions of cells and bring about physical change, sometimes instantly. And, externally, how the Mind creates new realities and is part of the process of creation itself. But our Mind's talent for creation doesn't stop there. Let's move away from theory and look at some actual examples of Mind Power.

Apparently, it has the ability to produce functioning beings separate from itself like, for instance:

Tulpas

In some cultures it is accepted without question that we can create an entity which seems to have a Mind of its own. There are hundreds of examples but one that illustrates the point well is that chronicled by Alexandra David-Neel, one of

17

those extraordinary women of the late 19th and early 20th Centuries who journeyed alone to live with remote tribes or cultures.

It was in Tibet where she studied the mystical subject of tulpa creation. A tulpa, according to traditional Tibetan doctrines, is an entity brought to life by an act of imagination, rather like the fictional characters of a novelist, except that tulpas are not written down but appear as three-dimensional 'living' figures.

David-Neel became so interested in the concept that she decided to try to create one herself. And she succeeded. Apparently, people who came into contact with Neel reported an attractive young monk in her presence that seemed to be a servant of some kind. As time went on, the attractive young monk started to transform into an overweight, foul-mouthed pervert that tried to make Neel's life a misery.

It is worth quoting verbatim here from her book *Magic and Mystery in Tibet* (University Books 1965):

'However interested we may feel in the other strange accomplishments with which Tibetan adepts of the secret lore are credited, the creation of thought forms seems by far the most puzzling.

'Phantoms, as Tibetans describe them, and those that I have myself seen, do not resemble the apparitions which are said to occur during spiritualist séances. As I have said, some apparitions are created on purpose either by a lengthy process...Or, in the case of proficient adepts, instantaneously or almost instantaneously. In other cases, apparently, the author of the phenomenon generates it unconsciously, and is not even in the least aware of the apparition being seen by others.'

She goes on, 'However, the practice is considered as fraught with danger for everyone who has not reached a high mental and spiritual degree of enlightenment and is not fully aware of the nature of the psychic forces at work in the process. Once the tulpa is endowed with enough vitality to be capable of playing the part of a real being, it tends to free itself from its maker's control. This, say Tibetan occultists, happens nearly mechanically, just as the child, when his body is completed and able to live apart, leaves its mother's womb.

'Sometimes the phantom becomes a rebellious son and one hears of uncanny struggles that have taken place between magicians and their creatures, the former being severely hurt or even killed by the latter. Tibetan magicians also relate cases in which the tulpa is sent to fulfil a mission, but does not come back and pursues its peregrinations as a half-conscious, dangerously mischievous puppet.

'The same thing, it is said, may happen when the maker of the tulpa dies before having dissolved it. Yet, as a rule, the phantom either disappears suddenly at the death of the magician or gradually vanishes like a body that perishes for want of food. On the other hand, some tulpas are expressly intended to survive their creator and are specially formed for that purpose.'

David-Neel then gives an account of her own attempt to create a tulpa. 'In order to avoid being influenced by the forms of the Lamaist deities, which I saw daily around me in paintings and images, I chose for my experiment a most insignificant character: a Monk, short and fat, of an innocent and jolly type.

'I shut myself in tsams (occult rituals) and proceeded to perform the prescribed concentration of thought and other rites. After a few months the phantom Monk was formed. His form grew gradually, fixed and lifelike looking. He became a kind of guest, living in my apartment. I then broke my seclusion and started for a tour, with my servants and tents.

'The Monk included himself in the party. Though I lived in the open, riding on horseback for miles each day, the illusion persisted. I saw the fat tulpa; now and then it was not necessary for me to think of him to make him appear. The phantom performed various actions of the kind that are natural to travellers and that I had not commanded. For instance, he walked, stopped, looked around him.

'The illusion was mostly visual, but sometimes I felt as if a robe was lightly rubbing against me, and once a hand seemed to touch my shoulder. The features which I had imagined, when building my phantom, gradually underwent a change. The fat, chubby-cheeked fellow grew leaner, his face assumed a vaguely mocking, sly, malignant look. He became more troublesome and bold. In brief, he escaped my control.

'I ought to have let the phenomenon follow its course. Once, a herdsman who brought me a present of butter, saw the tulpa in my tent and took it for a living lama. But the presence of that unwanted companion began to prove trying to my nerves; it turned into a "day-nightmare." Moreover, I was beginning to plan my journey to Lhasa and needed a quiet brain devoid of other preoccupations, so I decided to dissolve the phantom. I succeeded, but only after six months of hard struggle. My Mind-creature was tenacious of life.

'There is nothing strange in the fact that I may have created my own hallucination. The interesting point is that in these cases of materialization, others see the thought-forms that have been created.'

David-Neel's story indicates the ability of thought itself to take on a more permanent form, leave the control of the creator and assume a life and intelligence of its own. And then put up quite a fight to maintain its existence. This would suggest that we should be extremely careful of what thoughts we have. It sounds as if it is much safer, and more likely to contribute to the well being of the planet, if we think constructively. And think only kind thoughts of our fellow human beings.

Another example of Minds creating a being of some sort is the well documented tale of Phillip the Ghost. In the 1970s, a group of Canadian parapsychologists experimented to see if they could create a phantom, proving their theory that the human Mind can produce spirits through expectation, imagination and visualization. The group of between 8-10 people met regularly. First they agreed a fictional back-story for a 17th Century aristocrat who they called Phillip. Then they had practice sessions where they would meditate to try to conjure Phillip up.

You have to give them full marks for persistence because they kept at it for a year without any success. So they switched tactics, using a séance formula but with some major differences. No-one would be the lead medium and they would keep the room well lit. At last an invisible entity began to make itself known. Using a system of knocks for Yes and No, they began to quiz Phillip, who would give them answers along the lines of his biographical details.

The seance room table creaked, groaned and moved around without human intervention. As the weeks went by it would perform more startling actions, like rushing to greet a newcomer, chase someone round the room and distort itself by raising only one of its legs. On one occasion it even 'bit' a participant by trapping part of her hand between the two edges of its corner joint.

So, although 'Phillip' never reached the stage of physical manifestation, an entity of sorts had been created, just by the 'Intent' of human Minds. Now we've laid the foundations of why our Minds are so powerful let's look at some of the requirements needed to focus that power.

In this chapter you seem to be saying that I am capable of actually creating an independent-thinking entity separate from myself.

Yes, theoretically it's possible. However, as you've read from both examples above it took immense effort and time which most people – including, I venture to suggest, you – just won't have the discipline to do. However, it shows how potentially powerful our thoughts are as they don't need to be manifested as a phantom being to have an effect.

Do you mean our thoughts take on a life of their own once they've been conceived?

Very much so. Once they emerge from our Minds thoughts have the ability to wing their way to any place or time and influence what's there. That's why prayer can affect the past, present or future. We look at this counter-intuitive phenomenon later under the heading of retro-causality. And that's why we should be so careful to think positive as this can be constantly adding to the beneficial energies of the planet.

And, I suppose, thinking negative thoughts adds to the detrimental energies?

Right.

Things are getting weirder by the minute.

Let's move on and look at a couple of the ways we can focus that thought – and not create a ghostly being! We can use our:

Intent

The secret of manifesting your objective is start with an intent. And then to feel as if you have already achieved it. Paradoxically, straining every mental sinew to achieve an objective can be counter-productive as the straining tends to reinforce the notion that you haven't achieved something!

Dean Radin, Senior Scientist at the Institute of Noetic Sciences in Pwtaluma, California, suggests that a confident expectation enhances the effect of intention. All complimentary therapies have one thing in common: the practitioners' *intention.*

Another way of turbo-charging our thoughts is through:

Belief

In their book *Remarkable Recovery,* which deals with patients diagnosed as terminally ill who manage to survive against the odds, Caryle Hirshberg and Marc Ian Barasch conclude that of the hundreds of cases they reviewed they still don't know what the common factor is. However, after reading their material and looking at it from a different angle, a common theme seems to be the person's BELIEF that triggers their immune system (or even the belief of their medic).

This would explain why different protocols work with different people – the common factor is BELIEF in the treatment or their doctor (a powerful manifestation of this is the 'placebo effect,' which we look at later). So, that's why some healers take the view, 'If you don't know the answer, make it up.' Because it's the patient's *belief* in an ultimate solution for their condition that does the curing. And it's a two-way belief, too, from the healer to the healee and vice-versa.

This all testifies to the power of the Mind.   Even with those terminally ill patients who gave up and accepted their fate, but yet survived, it could be said it was their belief that kept them going - not in the therapy, or even the therapist but in an overarching conviction that 'All will be well.'

The energy of the mind is the essence of life - Aristotle

4 SINCE MY NEW HEART I'M A DIFFERENT PERSON

We've talked a lot so far about the power of the Mind. But, where, exactly, is our Mind located? Is it in the brain? Is it a kind of super-self linked by an invisible cord to what's in our head? Or is the Mind made up from the millions of cells in our body which, like termites, can act both independently and as a group? Some believe the heart has a greater power over the functioning of our body than the brain.

Similar to the phenomenon of DID (Dissociative Identity Disorder) is something called Cellular Memory Syndrome. This is where the recipients of organ transplants take on the characteristics of the donor. This anomaly was brought to the attention of a mass audience by the Discovery Health Channel in a programme called *'Transplanting Memories'* in which it recorded a variety of examples where so-called cellular memory altered lives.

27

In one amazing story an eight-year-old girl, who received the heart of a murdered 10-year-old, began having nightmares in which she relived the crime. Eventually, her dreams helped police track down the murderer.

In another story a shy, reserved woman has vivid dreams about the donor, even though she had never met this person. She also develops a more assertive personality. A third heart recipient strangely picks up his donor's musical tastes.

Then there was a woman called Claire who received a heart and lung transplant and, like many cellular memory cases, after the operation started to behave oddly (for her, at least). She began to crave beer and chicken nuggets, neither of which she had a taste for prior to the transplant. She later tracked down who her donor was – it turned out his favourite food was chicken nuggets. In fact he had just purchased a portion prior to being involved in a motorcycle accident and these nuggets were found inside his motorcycle jacket.

Finally, a 47-year-old man received the heart of a 17-year-old. Shortly after the transplant the recipient was astonished by his newly found love of classical music. The recipient of the heart found out that his donor absolutely loved classical music and played the violin. Indeed, the donor had died in a drive-by shooting clutching his violin case to his chest. Various experts in the programme explained why they believe cellular memories are transplanted with organs.

Dr Candace Pert, a professor at Georgetown University, said she believes the Mind is not just in the brain, but also exists throughout the body. This school of thought could explain such strange transplant experiences.

She said, 'The Mind and body communicate with each other through chemicals known as peptides. These peptides are found in the brain as well as in the stomach, the muscles and all of our major organs. I believe that memory can be accessed anywhere in the peptide/receptor network. For instance, a memory associated with food may be linked to the pancreas or liver, and such associations can be transplanted from one person to another.'

Indeed, a German neurologist, Leopold Auerbach, discovered over 100 years ago that a complex network of nerve cells, very like those of the human brain, exists in the intestine. Professor Wolfgang Prinz, of the Max Planck Institute for Psychological Research, Munich, recently wrote about this 'second brain' in Geo, a German science magazine.

Prinz said the digestive tract is made up of a knot of about 100 billion brain nerve cells, more than found in the spinal cord. The article suggested the cells may save information on physical reactions to mental processes and give out signals to influence later decisions. It may also be involved in emotional reactions to events. Prinz joked that the discovery gives a new twist to the old phrase 'gut reaction.'

'People often follow their gut reactions without even knowing why. It's only later that they come up with the logical reason for acting the way they did. But we now believe that there is a lot more to gut feelings than was previously thought,' Prinz wrote. He said he thinks the stomach network may be the source for unconscious, or possibly even subconscious decisions.

From all indications, cells communicate with one another, passing memories on, even to future generations. This might explain why some humans have vivid memories of past lives, especially when under hypnosis, that were never lived. They are reacting to cellular memories of their ancestors, not reincarnation.

OK. I've now had time to research what you wrote earlier about the Mind's link with Quantum Theory. And that the essence of Quantum Theory is the Double-Slit Experiment. But I have now read that the validity of this experiment has been debunked which surely makes your entire proposition false?

As with all scientific breakthroughs there are always the naysayers and the Double-Slit Experiment is no exception. I think what you might have heard is the contention that it is not the presence of the conscious observer that collapses the wave function, it's the actions they perform on the system that causes it.

However, those protagonists, who are a small minority, seem to ignore the simple fact that in order to perform an action, the Mind has to be engaged in the process. To be honest there have been other debunking theories but no-one has yet come up with one that has the validity to supplant 'The Observer Creates Reality.' And don't forget what Richard Feynman said – 'If you think you understand quantum mechanics, you don't understand quantum mechanics.' Incidentally, if you search that exact phrase you'll get about 16,500 pages of Google hits!

I'm determined not to be blinded by a blizzard of flim-flam. Let's look at another aspect of your case: We create a new universe every time we make a decision? That's just too fantastical a concept for ordinary people to get their heads round.

I agree. But just because it seems impossible doesn't mean it can't be true. Most people have got better things to do than worry about the esoteric preoccupations of quantum physicists. But, don't forget it's these esoteric preoccupations with all things quantum that have given us today's semiconductor electronics, lasers, atomic clocks, and magnetic resonance scanners to name but a few practical applications. The Many Worlds Theory is just that – a theory - but it makes sense of some aspects of the quantum sphere and that's all we need for now.

Hmmm! I guess that'll have to do at this stage. But, what you're writing about seems just a bit too far out for my belief system. However, please carry on – I'm looking forward to seeing if you can convince me to embrace any of this stuff. So far the jury is definitely still out.

The snake which cannot cast its skin has to die. As well the minds which are prevented from changing their opinions; they cease to be mind - Friedrich Nietzsche

5 CURSES! I'M SURROUNDED BY EARTHLY STRESS

There are many threats to human existence that the Mind can protect us from. Let's have a look at some of these and then examine how we can use our greater powers to neutralise them.

To kick off let's look at curses. Curses are a kind of psychic attack in the form of deliberate or vengeful oaths. They are usually targeted by the Mind of one person against another with the intention of causing physical, mental or emotional harm.

Curses and phenomena like poltergeists are aspects of the more general occurrence of bad energy which dowsers know as something called Geopathic Stress. This is an umbrella term for all kinds of detrimental forces ranging from the negative vibrations caused by someone's bad mood to psychic attacks which can maim or kill.

Yes, your headaches, or your mother's arthritis, or the crime rate in Chicago or Glasgow, could be due to geopathic stress in the form of negative energy hanging about your home or the environment like a bad smell.

According to UK professional dowser and geomancer, Adrian Incledon-Webber, we are under siege all the time from up to 40 different manifestations of bad energy which can reduce our immune system and give rise to a variety of health issues.

He says, 'Many therapists will have their problem clients, people who never seem to get better. Quite often it's the home that's the problem area. I believe "Heal the house to heal the person" could be the most appropriate form of action.'

In his book *Heal Your Home* he adds: 'The phrase "I always feel better when I am away from the house" has been mentioned so many times to me during my initial conversation with clients. I am always staggered at how low people seem when they finally find me. They have probably been "under the doctor" for many months, or even years, trying to find a cure for what ails them.

'Blood tests have probably been run, antibiotics have been prescribed and maybe a second or third course with no effect. Once in the grip of these "earth energies" running within and beneath your home, there will be no let up apart from moving house or finding an experienced geomancer (earth healer).'

He says that with all the advances that science has brought, we are still missing the point. Living in houses and offices 24/7 is just not good for us. We, as humans need to be outdoors, to be in the fresh air as much as we possibly can. This is because geopathic stress gathers, and is trapped, inside buildings. 'The way we live our modern lives means that we are falling into the clutches of this ancient natural energy.'

His checklist of detrimental sources range from underground streams and mobile phone masts to curses and 'psychic cords.' Before we all get too paranoid about what might be lurking in the bedroom, he reassures us that we humans all have the power and psychic authority to neutralise any dangers. Incidentally, geomancers like Adrian often find that the most potent cause of detrimental energy in the home is the negative thoughts, words and behaviour of the humans who live there!

He says arguments, rows, ill-feeling, hatred, all imprint themselves on the fabric of the house and stay there to infect future inhabitants. Estate agents know these properties as 'divorce houses' because couples move in, their relationship turns sour, they get divorced and move out and the cycle continues with the new owners.

Let's drill down a bit deeper into geopathic stress and how to combat it. Firstly, the word 'geopathic' comes from 'geo' meaning 'Earth' and 'pathos' meaning disease. These days it covers both naturally occurring, and man-made, phenomena that cause problems for us and our environment. Some of it can be radiation that rises up through the earth and is then distorted by weak electromagnetic fields. These are created by subterranean running water, certain mineral concentrations and geological faults.

Human beings can also disturb the Earth's energies. Quarries, tunnels, mines, polluted water and railway cuttings have all been found to contribute negative energies.

How Geopathic Stress (bad energies) can affect your Health

Geopathic Stress has often been found to be a factor in many serious, long-term illnesses and psychological conditions.

Research by Rolf Gordon of the Dulwich Health Society has identified that sleeping or working for long periods over a geopathic stress zone can cause sleep disturbances, headaches, anxiety and behavioural problems in children. Stronger geopathic stress has been linked to wasting diseases like Motor Neurone, Parkinsons and Multiple Sclerosis; also mental disorders such as addictions, suicides, depression and obsessions. And bowel disorders, including IBS and Crohn's disease. Other manifestations include ME, anxiety, migraines, cot death, infertility and miscarriages.

It does not mean that the geopathic stress *causes* these debilitating diseases, but if people have a weak constitution and are exposed to strong GS for long periods of time this can be the ultimate trigger that makes it happen.

When homes and offices are affected this is often called 'sick building syndrome' where the people within are fractious, moody, often unwell and generally under par. The World Health Organisation reckons that 30 per cent of all buildings are 'sick.'

Among the best known energy lines contributing to GS are those that make up the Hartmann Grid, named after German physician, Dr Ernst Hartmann, who discovered them in 1950. The lines, about a metre apart, form a matrix around the earth, running north to south and east to west, rather like latitude and longitude lines on a map.

According to Dr Hartmann, the worst place that a person can sleep, or work, is over a Hartmann knot, where two Hartmann lines cross, as harmful radiation is intensified into spirals, lowering the immune system causing health problems ranging from headaches to cancer.

Other invisible lines that can be detrimental are Curry Lines, a similar network to the Hartmann grid but ones which run diagonally. These can be aggravated by ley lines, (earth energy lines which connect sacred sites) and electro-magnetic frequencies.

Evidence Connecting Geopathic Stress to Illness

Consultant physician, the late Dr Hans Nieper, claimed that 92% of all his cancer patients and 75% of his MS patients were geopathically stressed. Dr Nieper was a world-renowned cancer and MS specialist and operated one of the largest MS practices in the world, located in Germany.

The German physicist Robert Endros studied such claims with Professor KE Lotz of the School of Architecture of Biberach, West Germany. Their analysis of 400 deaths due to cancer revealed that 383 cases were related to dwellings built over geological faults, underground water veins and disturbances of the natural geomagnetic field.

Symptoms of Geopathic Stress

The effect is gradual, involving a slow deterioration in health or performance in those who are most susceptible. Some early signs of GS are:

• Disturbed sleep, waking often, waking feeling tired

• Babies and children fret and don't sleep well

• Restlessness

• General tiredness

• 'Sick building syndrome'

• Chronic unwellness including ME, headaches, hyperactivity and some cancers

• A general feeling of something being not 'quite right' with a particular area or room

• Cracking or damp in a building that keeps recurring

I haven't forgotten that I said earlier that we have the power to counter all these energies and in Appendix 2 I explain how. Spoiler: it's another manifestation of our incredible Minds.

Causes of Geopathic Stress

Here's a list, by no means exhaustive, of some of the causes:

- Underground streams
- Energy leys
- Hartmann/Curry grid lines
- Energy spirals
- Electrical fields
- Electromagnetic frequencies
- Overhead/underground power lines
- Human energy patterns
- Human related energies
- Energies of conflict
- Mass consciousness (fear etc)
- Demonic forces
- Poltergeists
- Bad spirit possession
- Negative thought forms
- Curses
- Ghosts, spirits, trapped souls

Visible Indicators of Geopathic Stress

Cats seem to be immune to GS radiations – in fact they actively seek out the spots to sleep over them. Owls, snakes, slugs and snails, insects, parasites, bacteria, viruses, ants, termites, wasps and bees all like, and are drawn to, geopathic stress lines. However, to most other animals they are harmful. Horses and cows stabled over geopathic stress spirals may become sick or injury prone.

Some plants love geopathic stress. These include ivy, mushrooms, mistletoe, bindweed, foxgloves, nettles, docks and medicinal herbs. However, many fruit trees and plants will suffer. Twisted or stunted growth and gaps in hedges may be clues.

Bare patches in lawns, moss and fungi, stunted or mutated growth in veggie gardens can be due to siting over lines of geopathic stress.

Detecting areas of Geopathic Stress

While scientific instruments are not yet sensitive enough to register many of the harmful energies around us, Geopathic Stress can be detected by dowsing. A reminder: dowsing is an ability that allows us to search for that which is hidden from view. It is an ancient art that connects us to the Infinite Mind. Thousands of years ago human survival depended on the ability to find water and minerals so dowsing was a highly developed skill.

The dowser uses his or her body as a detector and the presence of energies is indicated by the movement of the dowsing tool. The British Society of Dowsers has a register of members who specialise in diagnosing and curing homes and offices affected by these detrimental energies. I give a 'How to' guide and a full explanation of divining in my book *Dowse Your Way To Psychic Power*. But before buying check out the reviews to make sure it's what you need.

You will have spotted poltergeist as one of the negative energies coming under the heading of geopathic stress. This manifestation is one of my favourites because it sums up the sheer other-worldliness of what we're dealing with. It's an extreme example of unexplained energy, seemingly out of the control of the Mind that produced it.

The word Poltergeist is the German for noisy ghost. In hundreds of authenticated cases from the 11th to the 21st Centuries impossible things happen which no-one has been able to replicate in scientifically-controlled conditions. Somehow, invisible energies start fires, move furniture, hurl stones, write on walls, smash crockery, produce knockings, speak in disembodied voices, play havoc with electrical appliances, and even produced a rainstorm inside a house.

Usually the phenomenon is said to be connected with emotionally-disturbed children, often at the time of puberty. The theory being that, somehow, the emotional turmoil is externalising itself without the knowledge of its source.

One of the most spectacular examples of this 'noisy ghost' activity became known as the Enfield Poltergeist case. Manifestations lasted from August 1977 to September 1978. During this time a mother and her four children, who were living in a council house in Enfield, London, experienced the spectrum of poltergeist phenomena. Over 1500 separate incidents were recorded.

Things started mildly with just a few unexplained sounds and then progressed to alleged possession and other more disturbing occurrences. It seemed as if a Mind was at work behind the phenomena because it consistently thwarted attempts by investigators to gather meaningful evidence.

In one instance, a toy brick was said to have materialised out of thin air, flew across the room and hit a photographer on the head. But the cameraman was not quick enough to capture any images of the assault. Many items caught fire of their own accord and metal objects bent out of shape.

The worst manifestation was the apparent possession of 12 year old Janet, from whom emitted a deep gruff voice. Janet was also reported to have been constantly levitated out of bed at night by an unseen force, effectively trapping her on the ceiling on occasions.

All in all the Enfield Poltergeist became known as a classic of its kind.

After studying hundreds of cases I have come to the conclusion that the highly-charged psychic energy is actually being hi-jacked by a lower-order entity who uses it to behave rather like a dim-witted hooligan.

Why it does this, and how, are two questions for another time. In the meanwhile, the important fact is that somehow energy given off by a human life is being manipulated by some kind of Mind to affect the world around us. So, if a person's thoughts, or emotions, can be transmuted to levitate a heavy object, surely the thoughts and emotions of us all are being transmitted all the time to either positive, or negative, effect.

And, the reverse happens and this is what is occurring today as armies of marauding negative energies are sweeping across our earthly plane, hi-jacking the human psyche.

And so to the 64,000 dollar question: How do we ordinary mortals – you and me – have the power to combat, neutralise and negate these seemingly unstoppable forces? Answer: by using the gift we have all got but don't know we have got - the ability of our MINDS to focus our INTENT and our BELIEF and, through the miracle of Quantum

Entanglement with our partner, the Universal Mind, reverse the negative effects.

All well and good , you say, but these are just words. How do I actually do it? As the response to this question is relevant to other sections of this book I'm including a detailed answer in Appendix 2.

By the way, the opposite of a curse is a blessing. And blessings work, too. You have the power to bless people, animals, plants and 'things' – even money. Blessing creates positive vibrations and these vibrations stay with the blessed. In crude terms your Mind can create what people might refer to as a lucky mascot.

Right, I've got a few questions – in fact more than a few. To my mind that last section's tipped right over into woo-woo.

OK, I'm ready to answer but I'm not sure there's going to be a meeting of minds, if you'll pardon the pun!

I'm serious. Reluctantly I'll go along with poltergeists as these are a well-known mystery but as for curses, psychic attacks and people getting cancer by sleeping over underground streams – if these things were real they'd be headline news. And 21ˢᵗ Century scientists and medics would have acknowledged this reality and come

up with strategies and treatments to combat them. The fact that they haven't must surely mean these so-called detrimental energies are nothing more than crackpot theories?

Unfortunately, most medics and scientists have an inbuilt scepticism about these kinds of things and those who haven't dare not come out into the open for fear of ridicule and damage to their careers. History is littered with pioneering ideas that were laughed at and their inventors ostracised.

Give me a 'for instance'

OK, for instance Thomas Edison's invention of the electric light bulb was called a 'fairy tale' by the British Post Office's Chief Engineer; the Wright Brothers' first aircraft was called 'a scientific toy of no military value' by a First World War general and, more recently Dr Barry Marshall, a gastroenterologist from Western Australia, was ridiculed in the mid-1980s when he asserted that that stomach ulcers were caused by bacteria and not by stress or spicy foods. He was later awarded the Nobel Prize for his work.

Put another way, strongly held convictions are often wrong: 'The earth is flat;' 'Heavier than air flying machines are impossible' (Lord Kelvin, president, Royal Society, 1895); 'The telephone has too many shortcomings to be seriously considered' (Western Union internal memo, 1876); 'Everything that can be invented has been invented' (Charles H Duell, commissioner, US Office of Patents, 1899).

There you go again – as I suspected, kicking up a verbal dust-storm. What's any of this to do with negative energies causing Motor Neurone Disease?

I was just trying to show that widely accepted perceived wisdom is not necessarily how the world really works. For all their intelligence leading scientists, chemists, physicists, physicians, surgeons, in fact all professionals, are taught their skills within a framework that rarely steps outside the conventional. Anything that impinges on this comfort zone is seen as a threat and closed minds clamp shut even more tightly. It's often the mavericks that are prepared to look at theories outside their ideology who end up advancing humankind's knowledge and understanding.

OK I accept that those who've gone down in history have been great thinkers, prepared to defy convention. But that's not really what I'm sceptical about. I just don't see how I can take seriously stuff like demonic forces or mass consciousness actually having a physical effect in my world.

Oh but it does. Think of it like this. As Einstein said, 'Everything is energy.' Most people see this as referring to a force that you can see and touch like hitting two billiard balls together and causing them to ricochet apart. But this kind of energy is only a sliver on the full spectrum of energies. Think of the electromagnetic range which stretches from radio waves, through microwaves, infrared, visible light, ultraviolet, X-rays to gamma rays. Light is a tiny section in the middle. All energy is the same but the frequencies are infinite. Put it this way: If I stood in the middle of the USA and opened out my arms to represent all scientifically measurable frequencies, the unmeasurable ones would stretch from coast to coast. Among these would be those we dowsers know as detrimental energies.

You're still not answering my question. I want to know HOW these unmeasurable energies have an actual physical effect. Give me some examples.

I've already mentioned some, like divorce houses where the negative vibrations from an unhappy relationship hang around and infect the next people to move in. Basically, these unseen forces do their work through human agency. They infiltrate the human psyche and bad things happen. A good example of mass consciousness spreading evil in the world today is the so-called Islamic State of Iraq and Syria or ISIS. Their physical influence in the world today is undeniable.

Yes, yes but this is just plain old evil spreading like a virus, as it does. There's nothing unusual about that. I want examples of these disembodied energies actually moving objects. In other words an invisible billiard ball knocking a visible one into the pocket. If I see that, I'll believe it.

How about a human body being lifted into the air without apparent cause? We have already seen how poltergeists can levitate people. But there are numerous examples of humans, without the intervention of poltergeists, levitating themselves (for the results of a study into this topic see the next chapter). One of the most famous examples of self-levitation is that demonstrated by the celebrated medium Daniel Dunglas Home who, despite conducting thousands of séances and being investigated on scores of occasions, was never found to have behaved fraudulently.

Tell me more.

Although his name is not very well known today, he astonished audiences, friends, heads of state, and the rich and famous with startling paranormal feats, including levitation. His seemingly impossible powers bewildered those who witnessed them, including respected scientists and journalists. It was in 1852 that Home first demonstrated self-levitation. Witnesses watched in astonishment as he rose a foot or more above the floor. When they tried to hold him down, they too were lifted off the ground.

In December 1868 Home gave what is perhaps his most famous performance. At his apartment in London, he conducted a séance for three respected gentlemen. During it he set the scene by rising off the ground and coming down again. He then went into an adjoining room and the witnesses heard a window open and shortly afterwards saw Home apparently floating in mid-air outside their window which was three storeys up. Home opened the window from the outside, then "glided into the room feet foremost and sat down."

We look at the results of a thorough investigation into this Mind Over Matter phenomenon in the next chapter.

I'm still dubious but I'll leave it there for the moment.

What I'm trying to do is give you real-life examples of the power of unseen energies which are all around us and working all the time. But we're just not aware of it because modern life has crowded out those aspects of what you might call the spiritual dimension.

In my opinion, there is no aspect of reality beyond the reach of the human mind - Stephen Hawking

6 I THINK, THEREFORE I AM

We've already seen how, in those people suffering from Dissociative Identity Disorder, the Mind seems able to manipulate matter and heal each personality of its malady as soon as it switches to an alter ego. According to Bruce Lipton, an internationally recognized authority on bridging science and spirit, whatever the brain (note: the brain is a servant of the Mind) perceives, it passes the message on to the trillions of cells in our bodies which then adjust to that perception.

You've probably heard of the placebo effect, but you might be less familiar with its opposite, called the nocebo effect. If the body is informed it has cancer it believes it. Told the opposite, it believes it. This is the Nocebo and Placebo effect.

For instance, there is the much-documented story of the man infested with cancerous tumours the size of oranges that disappeared 'like snowballs on a griddle' after taking a so-called wonder drug, which the man was convinced was the answer to his death sentence.   But when the drug was debunked as useless his cancer came back.

Then his doctor pretended an even more miraculous drug had been discovered and injected him with plain salt water.   The growths once again disappeared. A few months later the American Medical Association published another debunking article and the man died shortly afterwards.

Belief is the key.   Another example of the Nocebo effect is the true story of triplets who were born in the backwoods of Montana.   Because it was Friday the 13th the superstitious midwife predicted that each one of the girls would die one day before, respectively, their 16th, 21st and 23rd birthdays. And, because their mother unwisely repeated this to them as children, and their Minds believed it, they did.

If we   are governed by information fields, in which disease is just scrambled information, is this a case where the Mind is creating one of a million probabilities that exist 'out there' (the Observer Creates Reality)?   The Mind creates a scenario which is then projected back as a reality.   On the positive side, could this theory be used as a healing modality?

The Nocebo effect works with plants, too. In his book *In Resonance With Nature* Hans Andeweg tells of how he found that when he told a landowner that his trees were in bad shape they took on that bad shape from the moment of his diagnosis. And this gives us a vital clue as to where the energy comes from to bring about change.

With placebos we normally assume that it's the patient's own Mind that 'believes' something and that belief brings about a cure. But, in Hans Andeweg's case it couldn't be the trees that had the belief – it had to be HIS belief that was the governing factor. He believed the trees were sickly and they were sickly (as far as the landowner was concerned, his trees had been mostly perfectly healthy).

I don't wish to muddy the waters here but I suspect this might have been a case of retro-causality or backwards causation. This is a concept of cause and effect in which an effect (sick trees) precedes its cause in time (Andeweg's diagnosis). Reminder: in the Quantum World there is no such thing as time and space – all time is now. In fact Einstein insisted: 'The distinction between past, present and future is only a stubbornly persistent illusion.' But let's not go any further down that rabbit hole now.

From our contention that Andeweg's BELIEF played a crucial role, we could extrapolate that when a 'miraculous' cure happens it could be the belief of the medical practitioner that's as important as the patient's.

The annals of medicine are full of stories of unexplained and extraordinary healing. Often what all the disparate examples have in common is that the healing is preceded by some kind of profound personal change (remember the DID cases earlier?).

One doctor said, 'The patient who begins their journey is a different self from the one who ends it.' Recovering sufferers were observed to have had a 'dissociative experience' or had about them a'differentness' or experienced 'an existential shift' that set them on the path to remarkable recovery. Could it be that, by believing in creating a new self, the Minds of these patients caused a collapse of the wave function? And this brought into being a different self, one without cancer, for instance?

As I mentioned earlier in his ground-breaking book *The Biology of Belief: Unleashing the Power of Consciousness, Matter and Miracles*, Bruce Lipton documents proof that it's the Mind's perception of the environment, not our genes, that controls life at the cellular level. The Mind passes messages to the body's trillions of cells which act on those messages. If told you have cancer, the body believes it (the nocebo effect) but when told the opposite, the body accepts it (placebo effect).

In one experiment a group of cancer patients were injected with plain salt water. Thinking they were being treated with chemotherapy they lost their hair. In another experiment doctors found that the more dramatic the treatment the bigger the placebo effect. Big pills seemed to work more effectively than small ones. And even though the medication was inert it seemed to spark a physical mechanism as real as any drug. Not only did it relieve pain it also slowed the breathing and heart rate, just as opioids do. So be careful of the power of belief. This power is the reason that medical diagnoses often become self-fulfilling prophesies.

People often heal themselves when you have convinced them that healing is taking place - their unconscious Minds then manufacture what is necessary for a cure. It has been proved scientifically that if a treatment signifies care and hope to the patient, it often works.

This 'belief effect' isn't confined to healing. Addressing the topic of drugs trials, Bruce Lipton talks of the 'Experimenter effect.' He says that if the trials are paid for by the pharmaceutical companies the outcome is often in their favour. This is not because of cheating, but rather because the Mindset of the experimenters influences the outcome of the experiment.

He points out that 95-99% of our body is controlled by our subconscious, which has mostly been pre-programmed by the age of six. After that it needs to be re-programmed to counter negative traits. This would explain how emotional traumas experienced as a young child will often manifest in physical, mental or emotional illness much later in life. I know an 80-year-old afflicted with a lifetime of physical and mental torture until a therapist uncovered sexual abuse which had occurred at the age of six. Sadly, that client was only able to enjoy a few years of peace before dying.

I've heard about placebos and nocebos and I'm happy to go along with the power of positive thought. So there I was, thinking there was nothing I could argue with you about...until you get onto – what did you call it - retro-causality? Uh-oh, more mumbo-jumbo. How can something I think or do today affect anything that's already happened? That really is fantastical.

I'll admit it's counter-intuitive, but there have been numerous, validated experiments to prove it happens. And don't forget what Stephen Hawking said about the human being's natural scepticism. He said, 'We have no idea how the world really is. All we do is build up models which seem to prove our theories.' It is human nature to defend the familiar and to reject the foreign, even within science. A peer reviewer once rejected a paper on remote actions of consciousness, exclaiming, 'This is the kind of thing I would not believe even if it existed.'

I haven't the advantage of a planet-sized brain like Prof Hawking so give me a few examples I can get my head round.

OK, but we're going to have to delve back into the world of quantum physics. And, once again, introduce our old friend Prof John Mortimer Wheeler. By the way, Prof Wheeler is not a lone voice in the wilderness when it comes to his theories on retro-causality – he's supported by no lesser figures than Stephen Hawking and fellow physicist Thomas Hertog. Their concept of a 'top down cosmology' views the Universe as having begun in every possible way, with the most probable pasts *being determined right now* (my italics).

In contrast with the assumption that time must always flow in one direction, from past to future, this new cosmological model depends on the retro-causality idea that effects can precede causes – and this is on all levels of reality, not just in the quantum realm.

Back to Prof Wheeler for an example of retro-causality. He took the famous Double-slit Experiment one stage further, calling it the Delayed Double-slit Experiment. He used the light from a quasar billions of light years away, noting that it could be measured in two different ways – either as particles or waves. This is because the beam would be split and forced by the gravity of an intervening galaxy to go to the left and the right.

The scientist could decide, depending on his mood, to place two telescopes to check which side the light is arriving from. This set-up would be the equivalent of seeing which slit the light went through, thus checking the behaviour of *particles*. Or he could combine light from these two images in an interferometer, and make a wave measurement.

The mind-boggling aspect of this is the light began its journey billions of years ago, long before humans even existed and obviously long before the scientist decided which experiment to perform. But it would seem as if the quasar light 'knew' whether it would be seen as a particle or wave billions of years before the experiment was devised! Putting it another way, the scientist's 'observation' reached back through time to create the 'reality' of the light source (the quasar).

Although Wheeler's quasar experiment was at the time theoretical, modern laboratory equipment has enabled real life experiments to be conducted which have validated Wheeler's predictions.

You're still trying to blind me with science. I'm sure these boffins are all very excited about their experiments but I still haven't heard how retro-causality has any relevance for me or Joe Public. What's it got to do, as they used to say, with the price of fish?

Before we get to that I would just like to add a bit more flesh to the bones of the retro-causality idea. There have been numerous experiments to test whether the human Mind can influence matter. The simplest of these is to get someone to affect the workings of a random number generator. This is the 21st century equivalent of tossing a coin. Left to its own devices the machine will generate an average of 50 heads and 50 tails in every 100 flicks of the thumb.

Volunteers were asked to concentrate their minds and try to influence the generators to provide more heads than tails, or vice versa. One meta-analysis of the outcomes of these experiments, containing 832 studies and 68 investigators, found that people could indeed influence these random processes. The odds against chance was calculated at more than a trillion to one.

Taking these experiments one giant (retro-causality) step further, a group of Israeli scientists selected sixty heart patients in a hospital in the US and asked 10 faith healers to send distant healing prayers to a randomised sample. After a while a study confirmed that the prayed-for patients had better outcomes than the control group who had no intercessory prayers. OK, you might think, this is another example of so-called healing that abound on the internet. But the crucial difference here is that these patients' notes, indicating the course of their recoveries, had been made *10 years in the past*. The prayers had gone back in time. Or to put it another way, the patients' hearts had responded to healing thoughts sent from the future.

Wow! That is weird. Was it a one-off experiment or are there more examples?

Yes, there was the retroactive intercessory prayer study carried out by Israeli immunologist Leonard Leibovici. He identified 3,393 adult patients, each of whom had suffered from a bloodstream infection detected while they were in the Rabin Medical Centre, in Israel, between 1990 and 1996 - *four to 10 years earlier*. All 3,393 were randomized into two groups: 1,691 were assigned the intervention treatment and 1,702 was the control group.

The prayer for the treatment group was for their 'well being and full recovery.' The study discovered that their length of stay in hospital and duration of fever were significantly shorter than for the control group. Leibovici concluded, 'Remote, retroactive intercessory prayer is associated with a shorter stay in hospital and shorter duration of fever in patients with a blood-stream infection and should be considered for use in clinical practice.'

I have to admit you're starting to bring me round. But am I just being bamboozled by a few selected examples? There must be hundreds of experiments that prove the opposite – that the world works with a Newtonian predictability, except for a few wacky exceptions - like someone claiming to have seen a UFO?

Both sides of the argument can always find examples to prove their cases. In the end it's a personal decision as to which version you plump for. While you're pondering here's another thought to consider. In the October 2010 edition of the journal *Scientific American* Stephen Hawking and fellow theoretical physicist Leonard Mlodinow stated, 'There is no way to remove the observer – us – from our perceptions of the world...In classical physics the past is assumed to exist as a definite series of events. But, according to quantum physics the past, like the future, is indefinite and exists only as a spectrum of possibilities.'

And in their book *Beyond Biocentrism* Robert Lanza and Bob Berman say, 'Experiment after experiment continues to suggest that we – consciousness, the mind – create space and time, not the other way round. Without consciousness, space and time are nothing. This consciousness is co-relative with objects in that space-time realm.

'The conclusion seems inescapable: Suffusing the Cosmos is the realm of the Mind, whose observations cause objects to materialise, to assume one property or another, or to jump from one position to another without passing through any intervening space. These results have been described as beyond logical comprehension. But these are real experiments that have been carried out so many times that no physicist questions them.'

I'm mentally shaking my head in bewilderment. These ideas are all totally foreign to me and I need time to adjust.

While you let your thoughts settle, let's move onto a topic which is easier to get your head round – how our Mind handles different forms of energy which have profound effects on our lives.

The greatest achievements of the human mind are generally received with distrust - Arthur Schopenhauer

7 GOOD, GOOD, GOOD GOOD VIBRATIONS!

Sometimes focused detrimental energy like curses can be stored in an object and whoever takes ownership of the object takes ownership of the curse. Cursed objects are generally supposed to have been stolen from their rightful owners or looted from a sanctuary.

Power objects (bad luck)

An example of this are the stones from the Hawaiian volcano Mauna Loa. Despite warnings that this angers Pele, the volcano Goddess, Canadian Allison Raymond took some home as souvenirs. Shortly afterwards her husband was killed in a car crash, her mother died of cancer and her son broke his leg. When she returned the stones the troubles stopped. The Volcanoes National Park receives up to 40 packages of stones a day returned by scared tourists who had taken them home.

The fabled Hope Diamond is supposed to bear a curse and brings misfortune to its owner. Busby's stoop chair is another. It was reportedly cursed by the US murderer Thomas Busby shortly before his execution so that anyone who sat in it would die.

Power objects (good luck)

The phenomenon of the Power Object is repeated in Professor William Tiller's Intention Imprinted Electrical Device – better known as an IIED. William A Tiller is a professor emeritus of materials science and engineering at Stanford University. He is also the author of *Science and Human Transformation*, a book about concepts such as subtle energies beyond the four fundamental forces, which he believes act in concert with human consciousness.

In experiments he has conclusively proved that objects can 'hold' human intentions for years. Does it work on the same principle as the Radionics Box? This is the device where human intent is 'captured' and the intent is 'broadcast' - usually a healing command - to a destination target. We'll talk in more detail about this fascinating device later.

Meanwhile, back to Professor Tiller who, like so many geniuses before him, is seen as a maverick by the scientific establishment. For many years he claimed his 'abundant experimental evidence' was being 'swept under the rug' by his peers because it didn't fit into their prevailing paradigm (where have we heard that before?). Basically, they wouldn't accept that human qualities of spirit, Mind, emotion, consciousness, intention, etc., could significantly influence physical reality.

In an article for the International Journal of Healing and Caring Professor Tiller explained how conscious intent can be imprinted in materials, which can then be shipped to a distant laboratory where they bring about the intentional effect they've been imbued with.

A specific intention would be 'imprinted' into the host device via four very qualified humans acting from a deep meditative state. The device would then act as an effective surrogate. He goes on, 'The main target materials selected for this study were (1) purified water, (2) the liver enzyme, alkaline phosphatase (ALP), (3) the main cell energy storage molecule, adenosine triphosphate (ATP), and (4) living fruit fly larvae, drosophila melanogaster.

'By comparing the separate influence of two physically identical devices, one imprinted and the other not imprinted via our meditative process, we were able to demonstrate a robust influence of human consciousness on these four materials.'

He explained that there had been a measurable shift in the pH levels of the water as per the intention; the in vitro thermodynamic activity of both ALP and ATP increased by about 15%-30% (in complete accord with the imbedded imprints) and, finally, there had been a reduced larval development time to the adult fly state by 25%, meaning the growing larvae were more 'fit' physically and they matured more quickly.

The experimenters also discovered a totally unexpected and critically important phenomenon - that, by simply continuing to use an IIED in the laboratory space for approximately 3 – 4 months, the laboratory became 'conditioned' and the state of that 'conditioning' determined the robustness of the experimental results. In other words the space became empowered and its power remained with the object with no diminution - just like the lasting effect of a cursed object.

Professor Tiller concluded that directed human intention can affect physical reality. 'The space-time dimension appears to adapt to, and co-operate with, intention imprinted devices. Any IIED embodies an informational intelligence sufficient to fulfill the task set for it. The imprinted devices not only carry the intention of the practitioner but also goes further by enhancing the effect.' He adds, 'This is not understood but it happens anyway.'

If Professors Tiller and Wheeler ever met I would like to think they would have recognized each other as kindred spirits, both having arrived at similar conclusions from completely different directions.

Taking the concept a stage further I believe the IIED can pass on the intention to, say, a crystal. And a programmed crystal could, in turn, pass its imprinting on to water. For example, if it was programmed as a sedative, the water would induce sleep or relaxation in anyone who drank it. Or, the energetic patterns of a fertilizer could be stored in crystals and then transferred to water to produce an eco-friendly growth agent.

The polymath and prolific inventor Marcel Vogel, whose creativity and sensitivity led to numerous discoveries and product applications, believed programmed water would be the medicine of the future. 'Water,' he said, 'is the medium and Mind is the message.' He taught that water is the most programmable substance on the planet retaining the energetic signature of whatever is placed in it.

'It can record, store and transmit information within it,' he said. So the conclusion has to be that whatever has been imprinted on the water is absorbed by the human body after drinking and the vibrations are picked up by the body's water molecules.

67

The work of Masaru Emoto, a creative and visionary Japanese researcher, reinforces this idea in a remarkable way. Dr Emoto has been photographically documenting molecular changes in water caused by different 'thought vibrations.'

After exposing distilled water to different positive or negative ideas, words, music, emotions etc he freezes droplets of the water and then examines these under a dark field microscope that photographs the results.

His work clearly demonstrates the diversity of the molecular structure of water and the effect of 'vibrations' in the environment on it. The result is a series of photographs similar to those of a snowflake, each with its individual 'signature.' Dr Emoto came to the startling conclusion that water reflects our consciousness.

He followed up his research with a book, *Messages from Water* containing the results of his worldwide studies. The information and photographs in it are compelling evidence that our thoughts affect everything in, and around us.

Dr Emoto proposes that even as little input as a word, music or simply meditating on water vibrates the electrons. The resulting geometric patterns demonstrate the very real effect human beings have on their environment. By extension it shows how our awareness and observation participate in the creation of the Universe.

Dr Emoto and his colleagues took their experiments a stage further deciding to see if even words typed onto paper and taped onto glass bottles overnight had an effect. The same procedure was performed using positive and negative phrases and even the names of dead people. The waters were then frozen and photographed.

The different 'influences' they tried included the words, 'You make me sick,' 'I will kill you', 'Adolph Hitler', 'Thank you,' 'Love and appreciation' and 'Mother Teresa.'

The resulting images showed an identifiable response and distinct characteristics reflecting the vibrations that attach to the words. Those that had responded to 'Hitler' and 'kill' were ugly and distorted while the crystals formed in response to 'Thank you' and 'love' were beautiful and harmonious. Many believe this provides profound evidence that we can positively heal and transform ourselves and our planet by the thoughts we choose to think.

So if we believe Dr Emoto that human vibrational energy, thoughts, words, ideas and music, affect the molecular structure of water we have to acknowledge the power we have to affect our fellow human beings. Since the human body comprises over 70 per cent water, these same vibrations are having an effect on our own bodies, and those of other people, in the same way as they interact with water itself. That's why it's so important to be careful of what we think about and, whenever possible, think positive!

This is becoming a habit: I start off sceptical and end up half persuaded.

Only half persuaded? What are your reservations about actual experiments, conducted in a lab, proving that the power of thought can influence the world around us?

It all seems a bit glib. If the above is true – that Professor Tiller's experiments, for instance, are genuine - why haven't the results become better known? I mean if the experiments were carried out within accepted protocols, why hasn't his work been lauded and given due prominence in all the scientific journals?

Sadly, when maverick scientists produce any work that flies in the face of convention their peers rush to judgement and pour scorn on the results. Rather than do the experiments themselves, to either validate or disprove the findings, they take the lazy route and denigrate the work usually citing flawed methodology. This particular experiment prompted some fellow scientists, who couldn't find any evidence that the results weren't valid, to appeal on the internet for people to come forward and discredit it. Like this posting, for instance…. 'If anyone already knows of a good "debunking" of this paper, then please link! I wonder if there are a few more scientifically literate people out there that might be able to unpick what on earth this paper is about, and how they're claiming all this power-of-the-mind stuff from it.'

It's ironic really that Prof Tiller is a Physics Fellow of the American Association for the Advancement of Science, a distinction awarded for 'Efforts on behalf of the advancement of science, or its applications, which are scientifically or socially distinguished.'

In the end it comes down to who you prefer to believe.

A man's mind is stretched by a new idea or sensation, and never shrinks back to its former dimensions - Oliver Wendell Holmes

8 THAT STAINED COFFEE TABLE'S RUINING MY MUSIC!

Serendipity. Or luck, if you prefer. Luck can play a life-changing role in our lives. But, is it luck? Or is it us playing our part in some cosmic drama whose script has already been written and the cast selected? A discussion for another time perhaps. Meanwhile, was it luck smiling on audio engineering specialist Peter Belt and his wife, May, when they stumbled on what appeared to be the power of the Mind to alter our immediate environment?

It was a bizarre happenstance that led the couple to discover a unique way to improve the quality of the music coming out of their home audio equipment. It occurred during some listening tests when Peter decided to apply a chemical to remove a stain on their coffee table, which had been irritating him for some time. But it didn't work and the stain stubbornly remained so the pair decided to take a coffee break.

When they resumed listening the sound had deteriorated dramatically and had become distorted and jarring. Intrigued, Peter realised the only change to the listening environment had been the introduction of the chemical. So he removed the table to the next room and, to their astonishment, the quality was restored.

Peter brought the coffee table back into the room and the sound worsened again. They concluded that, in some strange way, the chemical had affected the audio output. After much experimentation Peter and May identified the chemical's opposite - a 'friendly' substance which, miraculously, seemed to 'overcome' the detrimental energies and transmuted the sound back to good again. Later in this chapter May gives a full account of this incident and how it launched a unique new business.

Meanwhile, many experiments later the couple realised it wasn't the chemical at the root of the problem at all but the human reaction to it which had caused them to 'perceive' a fall-off in the quality.

May explains: 'When we began to realise what was happening, that it was us (human beings) who were doing the changing not the audio signal, nor the acoustic air pressure waves, then we began to develop better techniques and various methods of applying the 'friendly' energy pattern to objects. We learnt how to induce energy patterns into various materials and this is the secret behind our devices and techniques.'

Peter and May claim that the audio from CDs and Vinyl discs could be transformed from average to superb, not by paying more for higher grade equipment, but by improving the listening environment.

Peter Belt is a supporter of Rupert Sheldrake's theory of morphic resonance. This is the idea of a mysterious telepathy-type interconnection between organisms and of collective memories within species. May Belt explained to their customers their belief in Sheldrake's concept - that as soon as anything exists a 'morphic resonance' energy pattern, a sort of invisible template, is created. As an example they would site the formation of the first Quartz crystal when the earth began to cool down.

The Quartz crystal, they said, has a specific chemical formula and a specific crystalline structure. According to Sheldrake a 'Quartz crystal morphic resonance' energy pattern would now exist. As more crystals formed the energy pattern would become stronger and this principle applies to everything - to both animate and inanimate objects.

At the end of this chapter, we look at Sheldrake and his theories in more detail.

Peter Belt believes that his products to improve the listening experience work because they alter the morphic resonance energy field surrounding the treated object. Changing the energy field of the object, he reckons, changes our perception of the object. Thus, Mr Belt's products change our perception of the sound coming from our audio systems - the sound is not changed in any way, it is our brain's interpretation of it that is changed.

But, could all this be bluff or honest self delusion? The common denominator in the seeming beneficial effects is May and Peter's INTENT. Did they imbue their foils, creams, cables etc with a cleansing INTENT and this intent stayed with the product and did its work (Like William Tiller's Intention Imprinted Electrical Devices)? If this theory is correct, could exactly the same techniques be used to create a healing environment, in which detrimental energies are banished by intent-imprinted devices or objects? Or, indeed, could we humans use our intent to change anything?

If you are sceptical about the Belts' unique theories, here's a chance to try the principle out for yourself. On their business website http://www.pwbelectronics.co.uk the Belts give these free sound-improving techniques (I have paraphrased them – more details on the site):

Plain piece of paper under one of four feet

Place a plain piece of paper under any ONE of the four feet of a piece of equipment *even if it is not an item of audio apparatus* (my italics). Listen to some music for a short time, then remove the piece of paper and see if you can perceive the same music with the same pleasure.

Pinning back one corner of a curtain

Pin back ONE of the four corners of all curtains in the listening room with a safety pin. Listen to some music for a short time, then remove the safety pins so the corner is not pinned back and see if you can perceive a drop in quality.

Plain piece of Blue paper under any vase of flowers or any pot plant in the listening room

If you have a vase of flowers, or a pot plant in the listening room, stand the vase or the plant pot on a plain piece of BLUE paper. Listen to some music for a short time, then remove the paper and see if you can listen to the same music with the same pleasure.

Tying a Reef knot

If you have two adjacent power cords, or two adjacent interconnects, unplug the power cords from their sockets, tie a reef knot in them, replace the plugs back in their sockets and listen for a short time to some music. Then untie the reef knot and see if you discern a drop in quality. If you have no adjacent cables, you can tie a reef knot in only one cable by forming a U shape, giving you two parallel sides of wire with which to make a reef knot. If you find that you have experienced better sound from making only one reef knot in one cable, then tie one reef knot in as many other cables (power or interconnect) as you can. This applies to ANY cable belonging to ANY equipment – not just to audio equipment. Warning: No other knots should be used - only a reef knot. Just make sure you do not make a granny knot by mistake!

Peter and May finish with this entreaty (with which I whole-heartedly agree): 'I hope by now you are beginning to be convinced of the notion that thought energy has an awesome power and that each of us has a great responsibility to use that power for the benefit of our fellow travellers, and the world we are passing on to our children.'

Peter and May are not the only people whose world view has been changed by Rupert Sheldrake. In his book *The Presence of The Past*, Sheldrake proposes the idea of Morphogenetic (structure-creating) fields in his Hypothesis of Formative Causation. In outline, this theory proposes that there is an information field unique to every structure or concept, whether it is a form in one of the kingdoms of nature or the knowledge of how to speak a language.

This field organises the basic physical material (e.g. DNA) or provides the unseen impetus or tradition which enables any new skill to be learned more easily by fresh generations of learners. The strength of the field is reinforced or even increased by usage and the field is adapted or evolves as new means of usage, or different events occur. Conversely, the field strength decreases from lack of usage; multiple and often nested fields exist for complex structures, such as human or animal bodies.

Although Sheldrake's theory was rejected and even ridiculed by some conventional scientists, it makes sense that the morphogenetic field includes the etheric and other subtle energies worked on by therapists like the radionics practitioner (more on this fascinating form of treatment later) who use their instruments to adjust the morphic field. The practitioner does this by comparing the present state of the patient with the ideal archetypal form and then attempts to convert the patient as far as possible to the Creator's intended 'perfection'. (We might interpret this as the practitioner's Mind collapsing the wave function and inviting in a different reality).

I believe all healing systems have their own morphic field – the knowledge and experience of everyone who has practised any discipline, or science, are available to anyone who has created a bond with that modality. And the key is to resonate with something so completely that you, in essence, become it. If it is done only half-heartedly it won't work. The idea is to embody it. Once you embody it you are linked to the power grid of that morphic field and you are in resonance with it. That is when the magic – the miraculous – occurs because you are linked up with an enormous, invisible database of universal energy when anything can happen. And you are working on the 'wave' reality not the physical.

Here are a couple of examples of a morphic field at work:

How do cuckoos manage to 'clone' the eggs in their host nest producing the exact colouring and speckled spots of those in there already? How do racing pigeons find their way home from hundreds or even thousands of miles away?

I believe these phenomena are allied to Sheldrake's morphic resonance concept. When the cuckoo settles on the nest to leave an alien egg some mechanism in the bird reproduces the exact frequencies (wave form in quantum physics) that makes up the physical egg and, like a 3-D photocopier, reproduces the same colouring and texture - enough to fool the host bird.

Similarly, a pigeon's base location comprises a unique melange of frequencies which the bird has absorbed into itself while 'acclimatising' to its home. Once released hundreds of miles away the base frequency 'calls' to its twin frequencies within the bird and the pigeon homes in on the direction. This is similar to a dowser finding the direction of an underground water supply, even when it's on a map!

The common denominator is the package of unique frequencies in both the transmitter and the receiver which are connected through quantum entanglement.

And talking of that mysterious quantum world – does the morphic field sit alongside the infinite number of probabilities already in existence? Probabilities, one of which the 'observer' brings into being? When he or she does is there a pre-formed morphic field already available to rocket boost the Mind's endeavours? Remember the doctors in the Chinese medicineless hospital? They didn't judge the cancer good or bad but said it was just one of an infinite number of quantum probabilities and they chose a different one, changing the quantum 'blueprint' of the infected body to its archetypal template.

This is a good point to remind you of a fundamental principle that applies to all our seeking: we will only succeed in our efforts if we are totally detached from the outcome. If we care too much, our ego is in play and ego is a huge Trumpian-type wall blocking success. In my experience this is one of the secrets of the Universe! The more the ego intrudes, the more likely things are to go haywire.

A degree of detachment from the desired outcome works wonders. Let Go and Let God, as they say. In fact I'd go further and suggest that cultivating an 'unselfconsciousness' puts you in tune with the Infinite Mind and allows your life to assume the meaning intended for it.

Before we get too far into the spiritual thickets, let's get back to Mind and Matter. Someone who agreed with the concept of changing matter was theoretical physicist Max Planck who once famously said, 'I regard matter as a derivative of consciousness.' He thought the trick to creating matter was to organize the energy. And what, he asked, organizes energy? The Mind – which collapses the wave function and brings into being just one new reality from the realm of all possibilities.

We've now gone so far down your rabbit hole that we've met up with Alice in Wonderland. Tie a reef knot to improve audio quality? Or how about pin back the corner of a curtain? Better still, stand a flower pot on a blue piece of paper. Come on...these Belt people are jerking your chain.

If they are they've done it very successfully. Not only have they built a reputable business in selling products designed to change the energies in the listening environment, but they have also persuaded some seasoned professionals to give them positive reviews in audio journals.

I just cannot believe that anyone in their right mind would pay good money for something that claims to improve the quality of what comes out of the speaker that's not even part of the equipment.

Who could argue with your logic? But logic does not seem to play a part in the Belts' discoveries. One of their products is something called Rainbow Foil, a strip of metal that you stick onto a CD. Here's part of a review by Greg Weaver in the journal *Sound Stage:*

'Let me tell you right now synergizers, you're probably not going to believe this. Hell, I'm not even sure that I do! It just doesn't make sense. No, strike that. It goes contrary to all common sense and scientific theory that I am acquainted with. But it happened! Those of you who know me, or have come to try the suggestions in this column over time with some degree of success, will likely think I'm a couple of cans short of a six-pack. But I swear, what I'm about to tell you is absolutely true, repeatable, amazing and -- to my satisfaction at this time -- totally unexplainable.

'Well, to say that my jaw dropped would be an understatement. There was just "more" there. It was as if some higher level of resolution had been unexplainably imparted to my system. Cymbal attacks were more clearly defined, voices more apparent, details more delineated, timbre more correct-sounding. Keep in mind, music fans, I was predisposed to discover that this stuff couldn't and wouldn't do squat and thank Mr Belt for his time! But I heard it. Spaces seemed more defined while instruments and voices took on new body and solidity therein. The whole presentation seemed more vibrant. I must be cracking up. It was just tin foil!

'Out came the "treated" disc and in went the "untreated" control disc. What the...? There seemed to be more haze to just about everything. Sounds weren't as defined, as focused or as vibrant. What the heck was going on? Back in went the disc with the teensy, tiny, little strip of foil. Sure enough, it sounded as if the disc had somehow been clarified! OK, out came the foil-treated disc, off came that bloody little foil strip, and back

ANTHONY TALMAGE

in we go. Damn! That heightened clarity was lost again. Time for a brandy. I had to sort this out…'

Well it certainly seems to have convinced Mr Weaver. I'd like to hear how you explain it with your mumbo-jumbo hat on.

I don't think there is any special magical quality to any of the Belts' products. However, I think they stumbled on the same principle that Prof Tiller spent decades scientifically proving – that the human Mind can convey INTENT to an object. In this case the intent was to improve the sound quality of audio recordings. With loving care the Belts transmitted that intent to all their products which, just like Tiller's Intention Imprinted Electrical Device, 'held' the energies. If you want to bring the Quantum element into the equation their intent caused a collapse of the wave function and they created a new reality.

It's a plausible theory I suppose. How do the Belts explain it?

Happily we know, thanks to a letter from Peter Belt's son, Chris, to Greg Weaver who was obviously desperate to understand the secret of this amazing discovery. As the letter plays into our own quest for knowledge about the powers of the Mind and energies we're surrounded by, it's worth quoting at length:

'Dear Greg

'My father has been working on a new (and literally "revolutionary") concept for several years, which has reached a quite advanced stage. Unfortunately, it is very difficult to explain in a few sentences how it actually works, but basically he has discovered that ALL objects in our environment have energy patterns that adversely effect our subjective perception of sound. This includes audio equipment! Thus, as we listen to music our body and senses are somehow "under stress" and our perception of sound is attenuated. I know that this sounds ridiculous and totally unscientific, all I can say is that new and challenging ideas do so at first.

'My father has designed some very simple looking easily applied devices, such as strips of "specially treated," sticky back foil that can be placed on any object thus negating the adverse energy patterns. The resulting change in the perception of sound quality is truly astonishing! Again I sympathize with your reservations but I strongly urge you to try these products out anyway.

'I would suggest that all the "Tweaks" presently used by audiophiles are not producing an improvement in sound quality through, for example, the reduction of vibrations as conventional theories would have us believe, but are in fact reducing the adverse effect of these energy patterns.

'As I mentioned before, the improvement that can be simply attained is truly astonishing. If you are willing to suspend your disbelief and skepticism and experiment a little, I will be happy to arrange for a free sample of one of my father's commercially available products to be sent to you for your assessment…'

So what happened next?

Greg explains to his readers his next steps…He says, 'Well, that certainly got my attention! Now, I'm not one to scoff at anything, especially when the jury is still out. But this sounded a bit too metaphysical or paranormal, even for this synergizer, and I openly stated my skepticism. Although I'm no engineer, I place most of my understanding in science rather than dogma. But, curiosity piqued, I asked for a bit more information. What follows is what I received next.'

Greg then quotes Chris's next letter, which goes into more detail. It was headed, *A Brief and Simplistic Explanation of Our Theory.*

'We believe that human beings have retained in some imperceptible way the primordial ability, acquired by life forms throughout early evolution as a survival mechanism, of recognizing threats of danger in the environment as energy patterns. When faced with such energy patterns, life forms then and now "go on the alert" or become "alarmed." As a result of empirical research, we have concluded that modern objects such as electronic devices, electrical equipment and plastics, are reproducing these energy patterns.

'In response to this, human beings have developed a way of modifying their physiological state so that we are able to live surrounded by these objects. In this suppressed physiological state we are unable to hear the subtleties of sound. Further more, through the work of Rupert Sheldrake and his theory of "Morphic Resonance" we believe all objects are "linked" and therefore, all adverse energy patterns are "linked."

'Our products incorporate beneficial energy patterns which, when attached to an object, negate the adverse energy patterns and superimpose beneficial "friendly" energy patterns. Our physiological state is then able to "relax" and we are able to appreciate the subtleties of sound. The more objects you "treat" the greater the liberating effect on our physiological state, and the greater the perceived improvement in sound quality.

'We believe the veracity of the theory can be "proved" very simply by attaching one of our products (e.g. a small strip of Silver Rainbow Foil) to an object in the listening environment not related to the audio system and experiencing/perceiving an improvement in the quality of the sound. Such an object (and this is only one example) could be the battery (or batteries) inside a remote control unit for a television or video. If an improvement is heard, there doesn't seem to be an adequate "conventional" explanation for it.'

Best regards,

Chris Belt

I must admit it does chime in with the idea that we are surrounded by energies which are affecting us all the time. Are there any more details about the coffee table incident that set the Belts off on their journey?

May Belt is a great advocate for their discoveries and has given talks about how it all started. In fact she explained it in detail to Greg Weaver. She told him in an email:

'During one set of listening experiments, we had a short coffee break. In the listening room was a small wooden table which had had something spilt on it, causing a nasty stain. Peter decided to treat this stain and applied a chemical to it. No success - the stain was just as bad. Peter shrugged his shoulders and said, "Oh well, we will just have to live with the stain, at least I have tried to remove it."

'After the short coffee break we returned to the listening tests. The sound was dreadful. It was absolutely appalling! Peter tried everything he knew but could not get the previous "good" sound back. He knew that the only thing he had done in the past half-hour was to apply a chemical to the stain on the small table. He took the table out of the room and listened again. The "good" sound was back! With the table returned to the room, the sound was dreadful again. Peter remarked " There is no way we can carry on with our listening tests with that table in the room" so the table was banished to the garage.

'We had no explanation for what had happened but we remembered this incident because it was so surprising and startling. It was a few months later that I happened to be reading an article - an article on plants! In the middle of this article it stated "and when the (???) plant is under stress, it produces the chemical ???? - this was the chemical we had applied to the small table!!!

'I read this article out to Peter and we looked at each other. Here was the chemical we had used being described as a "stress chemical." Peter then began to reason out "I wonder if it was us (Human beings) who were sensing this "stress" chemical and going under tension - and this was the reason why the "sound" was perceived as "dreadful"?

'He brought the small table back into the room and listened again - the sound was back being "dreadful" again. Peter began to reason out "If there is such a thing as a 'stress' chemical - could there be such a thing as a 'friendly' chemical? We did what all good experimenters do - we searched every cupboard, every shelf, every drawer, tried every chemical we could get our hands on. Nothing we tried brought the "good" sound back until one day, we tried Chemical X! This time, we judged not that we had the "good" sound back but that the sound was better than we could remember it being.

'Peter then began to reason out further. If applying Chemical X to a small table can "improve" the sound, what would happen if we applied it to other objects in the room - other items in the room as well as the audio equipment. Items such as a piano, a central heating radiator, wall lights, windows etc.   We did this and ended up with the best sound we had ever had!!

'Peter was devastated. You would think he would be thrilled to bits, but he was devastated. When you have spent the previous thirty years of your life trying every which way to get good sound and you suddenly find you have the best sound you have ever had - by applying a chemical to the central heating radiator, to the wall lights etc. etc. - then this is indeed devastating…'

The mind has exactly the same power as the hands; not merely to grasp the world, but to change it - Colin Wilson

9 WHEN I PUT MY MIND TO IT, THE TV EXPLODES

According to former professor of medicine at Stanford University, Dr Bruce Lipton, our unconscious Mind is a wonderful thing – it runs 95% of our daily lives and works without the knowledge or control of the conscious mind. Dr Lipton also says that the unconscious mind operates at 40 million bits of data per second, while the conscious mind processes only 40 bits per second. Therefore, it is the unconscious Mind which shapes how we live our lives.

And there we were thinking that we were in control and when we decide to take the dog for a walk, it was a conscious, rational calculation. But now we know there is a swirling cloud of influences in the submerged part of our mental iceberg that is really calling the shots. And often it is working away, like an aircraft's autopilot, keeping us on course while we get on with the practicalities. Sometimes, it seems to have (pardon the pun) a mind of its own. And it still finds time to play a key part in the realm of The Unexplained. For instance:

SLIders

How Do They Do That? A young man in Dublin walks past a row of streetlights at night-- and they go out, one by one, as he passes. An engineer in Woodville, Washington, is stopped by police and his car searched to find out what he's doing to their streetlights. An Australian in the entertainment industry parks his car in a parking lot, and the light above him goes out - until the following evening when he parks in precisely the same space and the light comes on again.

And how about this? When a guest in a restaurant in Athens, Greece, asks the staff to turn the music down, they refuse - whereupon the guest "kills" the restaurant's electricity and they eat the rest of their meal by candlelight. Other people affect traffic lights, computers, railway crossings... This has become known as the Street Light Interference (SLI) phenomenon. Once considered to be folklore - something that happened to a friend of a friend - today it is recognized as a scientific mystery with implications for our knowledge of the Universe, including ourselves.

In his book *SLIders – the Enigma of Street Light Interference* Hilary Evans cites hundreds of people who have reported their uncanny experiences, and he considers the wider implications of this fascinating phenomenon.

'It's quite obvious from the letters I get,' Hilary told CNN, 'that these are perfectly healthy, normal people. It's just that they have some kind of ability... just a gift they've got. It may not be a gift they would *like* to have.'

One SLIder told him that she regarded it as 'a ghastly affliction' because it costs her a fortune every year on replacing the electrical items that she constantly rendered useless. She added, 'Most people will laugh in your face if you're open enough to tell them. Over time, if they're friends, they will become sympathetic as they realise how expensive it is.'

No-one has been able to explain the phenomenon but there are clues. It seems the effects are not caused consciously. Some SLIders report that when it does occur, they often are in an extreme emotional mood. A state of anger or stress is often cited as the cause. SLIder Debbie Wolf, a barmaid, told CNN, 'When it happens it is when I'm stressed about something. Not really manically stressed, just when I'm really mulching something over, really chewing something over in my head, and then it happens.'

Another SLIder said, 'I went through a period of extreme stress after my daughter passed away - I became bankrupt, and everything was in a downhill slide for several years. At one point, every time I flipped a switch, I'd fry some device. We had to keep replacing light bulbs on a regular basis. I even came to a point of almost losing a job because I kept fouling up equipment and making track lights explode when I came into my office' (they were on a high vaulted ceiling, requiring someone to bring in a tall ladder each time).

'My most dramatic occurrence happened one morning when I'd had an argument with my husband just before leaving for work. I was fuming. Got into my car and turned the key in the ignition, and all four of my automatic windows started going up and down, at different rates. I kept punching madly at the control buttons on the driver's side door, but the windows wouldn't stop until I got out of the car. I finally found an online forum one day, with dozens of accounts by other SLIders. I don't think the site's still up, but what a day of confirmation, relief, and vindication that was!'

According to Evans a 'force' at work in SLI operates by affecting the voltage of the current, most likely by causing a surge that triggers the lamp's internal cut-off switch. 'To perform this feat,' he speculates, 'SLI would have to be an electro-dynamic force, somehow generated within or through the human biological system, and somehow externalised into the neighbouring environment, where it will act on any appliance which happens to be vulnerable.'

Evans writes in his book, 'If true... claims of SLI carry profound and exciting implications for science and for our knowledge of human potential.'

Levitation

This is another baffling phenomenon. It happens when the physical body rises into the air and then hovers or moves around, seemingly in defiance of the force of gravity. It's the stuff of science fiction but, for some people, it's a reality. Most scientists and academics have fought shy of investigating the phenomenon but a heroic exception is Simon B Harvey-Wilson of Western Australia's College of Advanced Education who has written a 258-page qualitative study. In it he states that all the evidence points towards some instances of levitation being genuine. In his report he says there appeared to be two main variable factors in levitation cases.

'These are whether they are voluntary or involuntary in nature, and whether the levitator hovers in one place or flies through the air. Joseph of Cupertino did both on different occasions.' He explains that, traditionally, most levitation reports originated from seven groups: shamanism, people supposedly possessed by demonic spiritual entities, those subjected to poltergeist activity, Spiritualism, people who believed they have been abducted by aliens, and martial arts such as qigong, and mysticism.

'Some people from groups such as shamanism, qigong and mysticism appear able to levitate at will, while people who are supposedly possessed by demonic entities, those affected by poltergeist activity and most alien abductees, appear to have no control over their levitations and are often thrown through the air.'

He says, 'These anecdotal reports generally describe levitation as rare, spontaneous and involuntary, although some people seem able to levitate at will…..The conclusions reached …. are that most members of the seven groups believe in one or more spiritual realms that contain entities and/or energies that can facilitate paranormal phenomena such as human levitation.

'Members of some groups (eg: shamans, Spiritualists, qigong practitioners and mystics) may deliberately seek to interact with, or access these entities or powers, while others (eg: poltergeist activity and spirit possession) may encounter them involuntarily.

'It also appears that, regardless of which group they belong to, all those who levitate, whether deliberately or involuntarily, do so while in an Altered State of Consciousness.'

Simon points out a curiosity in that demoniacs who were involuntarily levitated upside down did not suffer the indignity of their clothes falling down!

He says that some Altered States of Consciousness seemed to facilitate human levitation, and this was an important clue as to what energies were involved. He calls for further research into the capacity of consciousness (Mind) to access what appeared to be transcendent or transpersonal powers.

He concludes, 'To varying degrees, all the groups believe that Altered States of Consciousness enable people to access spiritual realms containing entities and/or powers that can transcend the known laws of physics. This suggests that the empirical sciences need to continue the investigation into whether there is an unknown, transpersonal force that links some aspect of human consciousness and physical reality.'

Interesting. But haven't you strayed from the main theme of this book – I mean what's switching off street lights, or floating off the ground, got to do with the power of the human Mind?

A lot actually. If Bruce Lipton and his scientific colleagues are correct and our unconscious Minds are carrying out 95% of our daily lives, these unexplained phenomena are included in that 95%. Which means we humans carry within us the ability to confound the conventional rules of physics. Surely, you must at least be intrigued by this?

I may be intrigued but these examples are so way out that I can't see the relevance for people like myself who I would categorise as normal.

But don't you see, they are clues to the super-normal beings we could become if we understood more and could learn to control these powers and switch them on and off at will?

Yes, but how likely is that? Surely you're just chasing rainbows.

Perhaps. But history is full of people ridiculed for their ideas who were later vindicated. And some changed the world. Take for instance Hungarian physician Ignaz Semmelweis. While working in the maternity ward in Vienna in the mid-19th century, Semmelweis noted that puerperal fever, an all-too-often fatal condition, appeared to be contagious - students and physicians were performing autopsies and then contaminating new mothers in the maternity ward who often died.

Semmelweis came up with a simple solution - that doctors disinfect their hands. And at the clinic in which his hand-washing policy was implemented, mortality rates dropped 90%, from 18.3% to less than 2%, in fewer than 6 months. He calculated that his discovery would save thousands of lives. Sadly, and typical of the reaction of the Establishment, his ideas were rejected by the wider medical community. To shut him up they ganged up on him and got him committed to a Viennese insane asylum, where he was severely beaten and died after 2 weeks.

You may not yet have persuaded me to get off my sceptical high horse, but you have convinced me that even the cleverest of people can be capable of collective stupidity.

But there have been happier outcomes for people ahead of their time. For instance Immunotherapy is now being heralded as a revolution in cancer treatment, but when immunologist James Allison first suggested his research interest in T cells, his mentors discouraged him saying that the immune system didn't play any role in cancer. And biotech companies repeatedly turned him away. Now medications based on Allison's initial ideas are poised to become among the most clinically and commercially successful cancer drugs on the market and Allison could still be in line for the Nobel Prize.

What you're saying is that today's ridiculed ideas are tomorrow's game-changers?

Yes. And the miracle and mysteries of our Minds are there to be explored and unleashed.

Human life is a great story written by the mysterious, mystical and magical human mind - Debasish Mridha, American physician, philosopher, poet-seer, and author

10 SEEKING A CURE IN A WORLD OF WACKINESS

A better way of curing people. This has been the goal of medical practitioners down the ages. And it has been the seductive claim of snake oil salesmen through the millenia. There have been notable milestones in this exploration, like the discovery of penicillin and insulin and decoding DNA. Meanwhile, complementary therapists have played their part, too, in bringing relief with techniques like acupuncture, homeopathy and reiki.

Healing sickness and disease is in everyone's interest - except, perhaps Big Pharma who are in the illness (not wellness) business. If someone came up with a formula that would cure all ailments Big Pharma would have to lock it away in a safe somewhere, never to see the light of day. Otherwise, their multi-billion dollar business built on pushing pills down the throats of humanity, would go bust. Sermon over. As I was saying, conventional doctors seek to restore their patients to full health. As do complementary practitioners, who use therapies without drugs to bring relief from the A-Z of human and animal afflictions.

In their contrasting ways, both sides of this medical divide are continually innovating new techniques and products to improve their performances. But they have all taken the stance that they bestow the healing – it flows from them and their skills to the patient with his or her medical need. But what if the Universe doesn't actually work like that? What if the 'laws' of the Universe are only suggestions? What if there's another way to encourage people back to health?

Here's a wacky idea - supposing it's the health need (say Irritable Bowel Syndrome for instance) that reaches out for the cure, rather than the cure imposing itself on the need? Supposing that all along we have been assuming that we identify the need and administer the cure while what actually happens is the need is in the driving seat, knowing the healing required and where to obtain it? To benefit from this off-the-wall idea is to BELIEVE in it. You have to open your Mind to allow that treatment to find you. Preposterous, you say.

This would require some sort of spooky intelligence to be working outside the known limits of science. An intelligence that can assess a situation and devise a course of action. But what if, instead of us sufferers looking for a treatment that will solve our health issue, we allow our need to invite in the treatment? And how do we do this? By BELIEVING that our Mind is already linking up with the right modality. And be open to what might at first glance seem a bit wacky.

Yes, some wacky ways do work. And if you are suffering from any of the thousands of health issues that afflict humans, wacky ways might produce for you a seemingly miraculous change for the better. Think of it not so much as a cure but more of a new you, with a spring in your step and a fresh optimism about the future. But before anything can happen it needs you to step outside your normal way of thinking and embrace this world of wackiness.

This would be the equivalent of what some eminent scientists had to do at the beginning of the 20th Century. Just to recap, back then, new thinkers turned the world of science on its head when they invented something they called Quantum Mechanics – the world of tiny things. Their theories swam against the tide of conventional thinking.

Now, over a century later, this revolutionary system is almost universally accepted and, as well as having upset Newtonian physics's 'standard model,' points us to a new way of thinking about healing people physically, mentally and emotionally. Before we look at this new approach let's briefly detour to remind ourselves what an upheaval these new kids on the science block caused.

At first they were scoffed at and ridiculed by their peers. Their ideas were the stuff of Alice in Wonderland, a realm in which the bullet arrives before the trigger is pulled, an object is in two places at the same time and two particles can communicate across millions of miles at a speed 10,000 times faster than the speed of light. Preposterous, they said. But, gradually, the scientific Establishment had reluctantly to concede their nonconformist colleagues were on to something.

We met earlier in this book one of the greatest physicists of all time, Nobel Laureate Richard Feynman, who said, (words to the effect) 'Anyone who thinks they understand the quantum world obviously doesn't.' Fellow physicist Niels Bohr, who pioneered the study of sub-atomic particles, agreed. 'If someone says that he can think about quantum physics without becoming dizzy, that shows only that he has not understood anything whatever about it.'

Reflecting on quantum mechanics some 80 years ago, the British physicist Sir Arthur Eddington complained that the theory made as much sense as Lewis Carroll's poem "Jabberwocky" in which 'slithy toves did gyre and gimble in the wabe.' Anyone who had shared these early pioneers' beliefs had quickly shared their pariah status. But the eminent personages in the world of conventional science were wrong and those quantum trailblazers who stuck to their guns laid the foundations for, as I said earlier, 21st Century technology like laser technology, the transistor, the electron microscope, magnetic resonance imaging, spectroscopy and fibre optics to name but a few applications.

So what has all this got to do with our world of wackiness? There seems to be demonstrable convergencies in both quantum and wacky phenomena. For instance, when dowsers find water hundreds of metres underground using just a forked stick it could be argued that, in the language of the quantum physicist, they cause a 'collapse of the wave function.'

As you know all to well by now this means the act of observing (dowsing) somehow prompts the energies that are floating about us as 'waves of probability', to become particles, which then assume a shape and become a reality. In the land of wackiness we can use this same principle to bring about healing. We can create a new reality. We can choose something different from the millions of probable outcomes. We can create a different person – one without the illness, disease or infirmity. We can bring about healing. In fact we can bring about all manner of beneficial change.

But as we now know, any meaningful change requires BELIEF. A refinement of 'Belief-is-the-catalyst' theory is the idea that even the BELIEF of a Mind *other than our own* can equally create transformation. Let's move on to a letter I wrote in reply to Stephanie, a reader of my book *Dowse Your Way To Psychic Power*, who wanted me to respond to a specific case she was experiencing. Her letter first:

'…Rather to my shame I realised that I had not finished reading your book and so completed the last few chapters just now… I enjoyed it and have written you a review which I hope is useful. I have one question though: I totally understand the section on the Double-Slit experiment, which I've read about and seen discussed on television etc. But it suddenly made me think - if a patient has a growth and we dowse to discover what it is, (with the question: is it a cancerous tumour, or benign tumour, or inflammation from an insect bite?) does it only become one of the aforesaid when we observe it?

'In other words, what happens if we ignore it? I know it exists because I can feel the lump or see the inflammation but… it doesn't have an identity at that point. (Don't panic I don't have a breast lump or anything - but I'm just curious in what you think.)

I responded:

'Dear Stephanie

'Your real-life illustration of a tumour is an excellent platform from which to look at the theory "The Observer Creates Reality." To answer your question I'll try, but probably fail (!), to be brief. First, to set the scene. I believe that the dowser (observer) "conjures" reality into being when he/she dowses. For example an underground stream 300 feet down. How can that be? That underground stream's been there for hundreds of years – how can a dowser, who's just stumbled on it, have *created* it?

'The answer lies beyond the laws of physics that we are used to – in dimensions outside of ours all time is NOW. This allows the human observer to help create the physical world we are living in. He/she does this when their consciousness causes a "collapse in the wave function" and one of trillions of probabilities posited in Quantum Theory, coalesces into a physical reality. Let's park that thought for a mo, and move onto how and where the humble human observer fits into the unfolding of the Divine Plan.

'Quantum physicists believe that the aforementioned probabilities are floating about invisibly and only manifest physically when "observed." Thus the dowser "observes" the underground stream and it becomes a reality. Or, as American theoretical physicist John Wheeler said, "The Big Bang happened because I thought of it and I thought of it because the big bang happened." Or, putting it another way, you "observed" the tumour and it is there.

'"No", you say, "my friend told me she had a tumour a month ago so it was already formed before I even knew about it, let alone observed it." And this takes us deeper down the rabbit hole. Because did the tumour somehow 'know' you were going to observe it and thus became a reality ahead of time? (Just like those particles in the double-slit experiment seemed to 'know' they were being observed). This phenomenon is known as retro-causality.

'Yes, human consciousness can influence the past through quantum entanglement, which goes backwards and forwards through linear time (don't forget, this makes sense if you accept that all time is now). By dowsing (*readers, see a full explanation of the ancient art of dowsing later*), you "collapsed the wave function" and brought into being one of the trillions of probabilities lying in wait.

'"But hang on a minute", you say, "I would never bring into being a tumour for my friend, so how do you explain that?" Of course you wouldn't, but you are not in charge of how the Universe unfolds – you are but a partner in the enterprise. As Shakespeare so percipiently put it: "All the world's a stage and all the men and women merely players..." But, are us men and women just playthings of a cosmic puppetmaster? And everything is pre-destined? Are we just living out our lives, unwittingly playing our part by obligingly using our consciousness as a catalyst for a drama already written?

'OR, is the blueprint just a shadowy outline which needs to be filled in by our free will, collapsing the wave function and "conjuring" events? If it's the former, then there's no use fretting about the tumour – it is what it is – a pre-planned growth which will either kill your friend or not. But, if it is the latter, you have the freewill to try to change it. If the tumour is malignant, you can heal it. "Hmmm!" You reply, "I'd love to heal my friend's tumour but if the best of modern medicine can't do it, how can I?"

'Answer: by creating a new reality!

'That's what is so exciting about the Quantum World – the unfolding creation of the Universe is a partnership between human Minds and the Cosmic Consciousness and is therefore fluid. Don't believe me? So, how do you explain the phenomena encountered in those who suffer with Dissociative Identity Disorder (previously known as Multiple Personality Disorder)?

'In her book *Fractals of God* Kathy Forti talks of a client called Valerie who had no fewer than 100 "personalities" in her – some male, some female, some a wild child. Some spoke a different language, some were left-handed, some right-handed, some needed spectacles, others had perfect eyesight. Some had allergies, some not. One was diagnosed as having cancer of the cervix but another was cancer-free. This suggests that anyone afflicted with a medical condition could cure themselves by becoming "a different person."

'How can the same human being have blue eyes and then, in another personality, green eyes? Or one has diabetes and the other doesn't. Or another is short-sighted needing glasses and the other has perfect sight? I know this is mostly a mental health issue but my point is the MIND *believes* the person has blue eyes, or green, or has diabetes or doesn't. The strong belief causes a collapse in the wave function and a new reality is created each time.

'So, create a new reality – your friend without a lump. This is basically what successful healers do. They visualise their patient without a tumour, BELIEVE that the new reality has already come into being and then they let go completely (if they fret, or worry that just resurrects the old reality). Sounds easy, doesn't it? But so difficult to achieve. You need strong visualisation ability, the dowser's intent, confidence, belief and an off switch!

'Finally, back to the two alternative versions – human puppets or Minds with free will? I know every instinct with most people would be for free will (after all what is being human all about if it's not to stand or fall by our own decisions). But there is a case to be made for Shakespeare's version…As Macbeth said… "Life's but a walking shadow, a poor player, that struts and frets his hour upon the stage, and then is heard no more. It is a tale told by an idiot, full of sound and fury. Signifying nothing."

'In other words, we play our parts according to the script during which each one of our souls experiences valuable lessons which enrich them for a life in another dimension. This would explain your friend's tumour turning into terminal cancer and putting herself, family and friends through mental and emotional agonies – to what purpose? Perhaps to enrich all the participants' souls through the fires of earthly Hell.

'Which version do you go for? If you've got lost in all these thickets, I'll answer your question: "Are we turning the tumour into a particular type of lump once we try to identify it?"

'Answer: It is already what it is, so we are not turning it into anything. By dowsing it and 'collapsing the wave function' we have merely brought into being what has been lurking there as a probability (we might then be able to change it, depending on which version you believe).'

Now, years after replying to Stephanie's letter, I wonder if there is another version of human free will which would explain the above conundrum. Has it actually already been exercised by each of us when our soul chose the next life it will lead in order to continue its balanced development and satisfy the demands of karma? In its 'in between lives' state it would know what was ahead in its new chosen existence because its destiny is already set out in the Divine Plan.

Once it entered its new life, the soul would have no memory of its decision and would therefore face all the choices of its earthly life - just as we all do – and using its best endeavours to make a judgement. Each choice our Minds make plays its part in the unfolding Cosmic drama. We follow this through in the next chapter.

You've almost completely lost me. First we have free will and can make choices, then we don't have free will because everything is pre-destined. Which is it?

I've tried to set out the alternative viewpoints – we exercise our free will by choosing to live a life where it plays its part in a drama already scripted. Or, there is no script and our choices create the drama as our life unfolds. You choose whichever you are most comfortable with. But, just remember, it's all based on Quantum Theory which humans, however clever, just can't get their heads round.

I'll have to ponder a lot more on all this. Meanwhile, that's not the only 'clear as mud' bone I have to pick with you. I was OK with Big Pharma being in the illness business but you started to lose me with the need reaching out for the cure. You would have me believe that an illness has got some form of intelligence and can diagnose its own cure.

I couldn't have put it better myself.

But all this is just another example of how you're living in your own bubble – detached from the reality the rest of us have to cope with in our day-to-day lives. I feel sorry for poor Stephanie – what she made of your reply I can't imagine. Conjuring a new reality, a partnership

between the human Mind and Cosmic Consciousness, all humans working to a script...concepts completely alien to most people, including me. Wacky is certainly the right word.

So far you've only seen half the picture. If you stick with it and read on you may find some wacky ideas that will change your mind and set you on a new path of discovery.

Our mind will answer most questions if you learn to relax and wait for the answer - William S Burroughs, American writer and visual artist

11 HOLD OUT YOUR ARM AND LIE
IF YOU DARE

We briefly met the inventor, Hugh Everett, earlier in the book. His Many Worlds Theory now has a growing following among physicists who say it solves many of the conundrums of the Copenhagen Interpretation. This, remember, says that observation by a human Mind causes all possible states to collapse into one. But, according to Everett, every time we make a choice the Universe splits into two. He agrees that when a binary decision is made by human consciousness one probability does collapse into reality.

But...so does the other probability. While ours manifests itself in our universe, as per the Copenhagen interpretation, Everett's also comes into being – *but in its own universe* which has been simultaneously created by the human Mind. Thus as we go through our day, says Everett, we are making binary decisions, and creating other universes, all the time.

However, while we see what has happened in our universe we have no knowledge of what's going on in the others, in which duplicates of ourselves have conjured into being the alternative outcomes – so while in ours we marry, in the others we may stay single, get divorced, have children or stay childless etc. If Everett is correct could it mean that each version of ourselves shares an eternal soul which is being imprinted with ALL the experiences we undergo in ALL our universes. Rather like a hologram, each soul (because it is quantumly entangled) is acted upon by its 'twins' and as each impression is made they ALL change equally.

If you apply Everett's theory to, say, healing all you need to do is quantumly create a new, healed person who is happily existing in the bright new universe you've just conjured - your challenge is how to swop the well person in the other universe with the sick person in this...

'Wacky' ways work

I talked earlier of 'wacky' ways of healing. And health needs that are seeking the cures. What I meant was allowing our Minds to entertain unconventional methods and devices to achieve a successful outcome. As we open our Minds, the Universe responds by sending us what we need. Take the therapy of Radionics for instance. Radionics captures perfectly the concept of our Mind creating a new reality. What is radionics? It's a system of non-invasive, vibrational medicine that proved highly successful in the United States until the medical authorities, feeling under threat, outlawed it.

It not only helped heal humans and animals but it was also found to be highly effective in keeping crops healthy and was, until Big Agri intervened, widely used by farmers who found their need for pesticides had diminished to zero. Though outlawed in the US it remains legal in the UK and there are many radionics practitioners in the UK to choose from.

The UK's Radionics Association describes the system thus…'a healing technique in which our natural intuitive faculties are used both to discover the energetic disturbances underlying illness and to encourage the return of a normal energetic field that supports health. It is independent of the distance between practitioner and patient…Basic to radionic practice is a disciplined dowsing or radiesthetic skill. Experience has shown that in trained hands radionic treatment can be helpful in a wide range of conditions.'

One of the first proponents of radionics was Thomas Galen Hieronymus who patented his 'black box' machine in the US in 1949. He described his invention as 'intent becoming focused and realised through instrumentation.' He explained that the secret ingredient was the experimenter, who became part of his own machine, bridging the real and the psychic worlds.

Practitioners discovered a curiosity about the whole business of radionics – that is analysing how it worked seemed to inhibit the intent. In an experiment, sceptical scientists scored zero while pupils from the local high school, with totally open Minds, gained a 99% success rate.

In his book, *Vibrational Medicine for the 21st Century*, Richard Gerber MD writes: 'This developing science provides a whole new understanding of the far-reaching potentials of human consciousness and the hidden capabilities of the multi-dimensional human being.

'It is a unique healing modality - a system of diagnosis and treatment geared to more than just the physical body…. It may ultimately teach us the most about the vibrational nature of healing and consciousness itself….and aid us in releasing our own inner capacities for self-healing and healing at a distance.'

119

He adds, 'Radionics is also an environmentally friendly therapy. There is no drain on natural resources nor unwanted side effects.'

Practitioners use an instrument, based on Hieronymus's invention, to both analyse and treat the physical and emotional weaknesses evident in the patient's subtle energy field. The device usually has several numbered dials, a 'rubbing plate' and a 'well' in which blood, skin and other samples, called witnesses, are placed. An early proponent of Radionics, Dr Ruth Drown, diagnosed patients' ailments using their blood or hair samples and then treated them, remotely, using the same samples. She believed that the samples' vibrations were a reflection of the whole person.

The rubbing plate (similar in principle to the dowser's pendulum or rod) is used by the operator to discern a number (from zero to 9) while scraping his/her thumb across the surface. His/her other hand would be twiddling one of the numbered knobs. At some point a mysterious force causes the thumb to 'stick' and the number pointed to by the knob would be the correct digit. If the instrument has four knobs there would eventually be four digits. Six knobs would produce six digits...And so on.

The final number – say 6498 – would be the 'rate' - a kind of code which activates the healing process. The theory is that the instrument serves to focus the Mind of the practitioner and, once the weaknesses in the patients' subtle energy field have been identified, the specific healing 'rates', are 'broadcast' to the patient. The 'transmission' is not limited by distance, time or space. The essence of the system is that the 'broadcast' is treating the cause of the ailment not the symptom. Curiously, this was instinctively applied in the 16th Century when apothecaries would rub healing ointment on the blade of the sword rather than to the wound.

Are the principles of Radionics mumbo-jumbo? On the face of it, yes. But how do you explain the documented and confirmed thousands of successful cures achieved and crops saved from the ravages of pests like the boll weevil?

In his book *Teletherapy,* AK Bhattacharya dispenses with the rate and cuts to the chase. He writes of creating 'Cure' commands and treating the patient with them. He suggests the practitioner writes on a piece of circular card in red ink (the Belts' red pen has a similar function) something like, 'Mr X, cancer, diabetes, high blood pressure, CURE' and then 'broadcast' it to the patient via his witness (a sample of hair, skin or blood). What Bhattacharya calls the 'intelligent cosmic rays' will then be set into motion and perform the healing work, over a suitable time period. He claims to have obtained many excellent results by this simple method.

121

It seems to me that this is just another modality that creates a partnership between the Mind of the practitioner, the Cosmic Mind and the patient. The therapist's Mind creates a new reality and 'conjures' a cure. The 'black box' or device merely acts as an intermediary, perhaps both boosting the practitioner's confidence while at the same time assuming the role of Prof Tiller's IIED. We also can now allow the possibility that the Infinite Mind has caused the diseases (cancer, diabetes, high blood pressure) to reach out to the cure (radionics). Radionics has enabled a collapse of the wave function and brought into being a new reality (no cancer, diabetes, high blood pressure).

Some believe that the vibrations in animals and plants represent the electro-magnetic blueprint which lies behind all living things (the morphic field?) and that when the vibrations are 'sick' the outer manifestation becomes sick too. Cure this sickness and you cure the living thing. From a quantum viewpoint this makes sense. The 'blueprint' is made of waves. Collapse the wave and create the cure.

And Quantum Entanglement - a state of connectedness agreed now pretty universally by scientists – comes into it too. QE demonstrates that all sub-atomic particles (which make up everything in the Universe) are somehow connected and that any part of us will remain for ever connected with all other parts. That is why a spot of blood can carry the vibrations of its owner and how 'treating' this sample can affect the whole human being.

And like William Tiller's Intention Imprinted Electrical Device the radionics 'black box' seems to hold the intention of its operator and 'broadcasts' it. Early versions of the device used actual electricity but, gradually over the years, it became apparent that no potentiometers, no wiring, even no dials were needed for the healing to work. In fact we now know that creating a convincing-looking treatment device is only necessary in order to provide something for the patient to focus on while, for the operator, it helps get the ego out of the way.

For some practitioners who have learned to shed their egos all they need to do is come up with a 'rate' they believe in and the healing power will flow! However, the novice operator may still need the full black box procedure to reinforce the conviction that something concrete is being done and, with the dials set and the rate selected, *is continuing to be done.*

John W Campbell, Editor of *Astounding Science Fiction* Magazine published in the 1950s, constructed a radionics machine built entirely of paper with the schematics drawn with India ink. According to Mr Campbell, 'The machine worked beautifully and the consistency of performance is excellent.'

If he had been alive today he would have been a great supporter of William Tiller as he said of his experiments with Radionics, 'Purposive energies can saturate matter, as a magnetic field can saturate steel and magnetise it. I very studiedly saturated my symbolic drawing with a conviction that this would work by reason of the laws of symbolic magic.'

A curious factor which arose as Radionics developed was 'burnout' among practitioners. Many became drained of energy and permanently exhausted. It was discovered that those most affected were therapists who fretted about the process and urged it on mentally. This had the effect of switching the healing channels from the dimension outside themselves, which the black box provided, to taking on the healing role personally.

Well-intentioned no doubt, but by allowing ego to assert itself the human psyche was being drained. So, besides giving the patient and therapist a focus for their healing needs, the device was also acting as a surrogate for the healer, keeping his or her energies safe.

There are many other systems of healing therapy which use basically the same principles as radionics – that is addressing the resonances that lie behind the physical. These other modalities include Homeopathy, Kinesiology, Reiki,

Shen, Emotional Freedom Technique, Qigong, Life Alignment and many others.

Kinesiology is particularly interesting when it comes to demonstrating the near-miraculous powers of the Mind. Before we get to that let's look at what kinesiology is: It evaluates health by exploring the biofeedback from muscles. For instance, the client is asked to extend their right arm while the therapist presses down on it while asking a question. The arm remaining strong designates a positive while a collapsing arm indicates a negative.

The therapy was started by Dr George Goodheart, a chiropractor who co-opted the techniques of Traditional Chinese Medicine, including acupuncture, to set up a model of disease as a disturbance of energy flow in the body, rather than as a physical entity, and visualises muscles as linked to specific organs. Goodheart posited that a stress which strains the whole body can be discerned by the weakening of a single muscle.

The interest in muscle-testing exploded with the publication of a book called *Power Vs Force*, by David Hawkins, a professor whose interests included the philosophy of science, mathematics, economics, childhood science education, and ethics. He discovered that Kinesiology was not just a way of diagnosing physical ills but, more importantly to him, was an infallible way of finding out the truth about anything! It could apparently instantly determine the verity or falsehood of any statement or supposed fact. The blurb for the book explains: 'Imagine if you had access to a simple yes-or-no answer to any question you wished to ask? A demonstrably true answer. Any question . . . think about it.'

In the book Hawkins states, '...the human Mind is like a computer terminal connected to a giant database. The database is human consciousness itself... with its roots in the common consciousness of all mankind. ...The unlimited information contained in the database has now been shown to be readily available to anyone in a few seconds, at any time and in any place.'

Sorry to stop you in full flow, but I'd like to ask a question. Surely, if this is true Prof Hawkins has stumbled on a gift more precious than rubies?

I know, it sounds to good to be true, doesn't it? But, Hawkins has a huge following world-wide and has demonstrated the precision of his system. He claims that, by muscle-testing, anyone can acquire an accurate answer to any question (except predicting the future) by getting a 'yes or no', 'true or false' response, having accessed the sum total of human experience (some might refer to this as the Akashic Record). With his research assistants, Dr Hawkins performed thousands of tests confirming the reliability of the procedure.

Then he took things a stage further giving us all a way of discerning the positive or negative value of anything – a book, film, website, a product or a human being.

How did he do this?

Using muscle-testing Dr Hawkins devised a logarithmic ranking of different levels of consciousness, from shame (20) to courage (200) to enlightenment (700 - 1,000). Hawkins states that anything below 200 level of consciousness is negative, false, weak and therefore not life sustaining and anything above 200 is positive, true and life sustaining.

He claims everything in our environment (back to the Belts again) has an effect on our individual level of consciousness – people, TV, radio, books, places, objects, in fact everything. He contrasts Power vs Force in the areas of politics, the marketplace, sports and all areas of human life. The overall message of the book is that we have to avoid at all cost the things, people, places, products etc that fall below the critical level of 200 because they weaken us and they lower our own level of consciousness. At the same time we should align ourselves with everything that is above 200 which is positive, true and life sustaining.

And Dr Hawkins says you can tell which is which, just by this muscle-testing?

Yes. By simply pressing down on the outstretched arm of anyone while, at the same time asking a question. If the answer is 'no' or 'false' the arm will go down easily. But for a 'yes' or 'true' it will remain strong.

Wow! This sounds incredible. You mentioned checking tv programmes or books and stuff. How would this work?

To evaluate a book – say Moby Dick – you would get your partner to hold it in one hand while you muscle-test, asking: 'Does this book score a Level of Consciousness above 200?' Yes. Above 300? Yes. Above 400? No. Above 350? No. Above 325? Yes. You can keep on refining until your final answer is, say, 335 - almost at the level of Acceptance, Forgiveness, Transcendence and Harmony. In other words, a definite benefit for the reader.

Dr Hawkins says, 'We think we live by forces we control, but in fact we are governed by power from unrevealed sources, power over which we have no control. The Universe holds its breath as we choose, instant by instant, which pathway to follow; for the Universe, the very essence of life itself, is highly conscious. Every act, thought, and choice adds to a permanent mosaic; our decisions ripple through the Universe of consciousness to affect the lives of all.'

That is profound

When you become the master of your mind, you are master of everything - Swami Satchidananda

12 I DID NOTHING AND A MIRACLE STILL HAPPENED

Should we regard Dr Hawkins as wacky? He claims we all have the ability to either boost people's lives above the 200 boundary in his Map of Consciousness towards Love, Joy and Peace or below to fear, grief and guilt. And we can do this by just being us, interacting kindly and considerately towards our fellow human beings or behaving spitefully, selfishly or by being generally negative.

Those who would like actively to become a healer (if you are kind, you are a healer) might consider using a modality that suits your character and world view. Let's have a look at a couple more, both non-invasive but highly effective in treating physical, emotional, mental and spiritual ills. And watch out for the common theme – the effectiveness of our Minds working in partnership with the Infinite Mind.

Take colour therapy, for instance. Back in the late 1800s India-born physician Dinshah P Ghadiali was presented with a unique opportunity to apply his studies in order to save the life of a woman, who had been given up on by her doctors and was merely hours away from death.

When all other conventional avenues had been exhausted, Dinshah applied coloured light directed at portions of her nude body using a blue tinged glass bottle and illumination from a kerosene lantern. Within hours a miracle happened. The woman started to recover and, eventually, walked out of the hospital back to her normal life. The simple application of coloured light had somehow interacted with the pathogens to neutralise them.

In 1911 Dinshah emigrated to the US and started a therapy system which he called Spectro-chrome. Based on his India researches it involved exposing problem areas of the body to different wavelengths of coloured light. It worked so successfully that the American Medical Association, as they did with Radionics, froze him out and eventually persuaded the courts to close his practice down and destroy all his equipment.

You can find details of his 46-year struggle in *Let There Be Light* (see the bibliography at the end of this book) which also gives all the information you need to test his theories for yourself. As it happens I developed his concepts and combined them with the principles of homeopathy to devise a unique form of colour therapy which I call Intuitive Chromeopathy. If you are not interested in this skip to the next section but if you are intrigued to know about a non-invasive modality, which you could adopt to cure any number of human and animal conditions, read on! I've explained how it works with a Q & A format. And if you are inspired to use the system, feel free. I have waived all Intellectual Property Rights to enable anyone to develop their own practices as they see fit.

So what is intuitive chromeopathy?

It is a unique therapy in which the wisdom of the ancients meets 21st Century science

How does it work?

It would be easier to explain if we take one word at a time:

Intuitive means receiving information from the unconscious Mind, which is plugged in permanently to the Universal Information Field. It's how diviners find hidden sources of water for instance.

Chromeopathy is using colour to 'radiate' the energy body of a human, animal or plant, to restore it to optimum health. This is done by shining the colour via a lamp and specially-selected gel filters onto either all, or part, of the physical body. This same light is also used to impregnate pure water with the same healing frequency. Using a technique successfully employed in homeopathy a few drops are mixed into a full glass of water and drunk up to four times a day to supplement the effect.

Tell me more about the Intuitive part of the treatment

As I mentioned before, diviners use their intuition to find answers to questions that lie beyond the range of their normal five senses. In this way they can locate underground water or minerals, archaeological remains, trace lost people or objects, discover harmful energy lines in the environment and pinpoint the cause of some physical illnesses. Intuitive Chromeopathy employs the same skills to ascertain the perfect colour to provide for your current need, whether it be physical, emotional, mental or spiritual.

What colours are we talking about?

We use 12 colours – SCARLET, MAGENTA, PURPLE, VIOLET, INDIGO, TURQUOISE, BLUE, GREEN, LEMON, YELLOW, ORANGE AND RED. Science tells us that each of these colours is part of the electromagnetic spectrum which ranges from radio waves at one end to gamma rays at the other.

Why are these particular colours so special?

They are the visible part of the spectrum with violet at 400 nanometres through to red at 780 nanometres. And each colour in itself has a mini-spectrum of frequencies. All sentient beings need light to maintain health. Normally the frequency required by the body is filtered naturally from sunlight but if there is a health imbalance colours – which are really frequencies - need to be provided individually.

What proof is there that ordinary coloured light has any physical effect on anything, let alone a human body?

No less a person than Albert Einstein, famous for his Theory of Relativity, proved that ordinary light has a physical action. In fact he won his Nobel Prize, not for his equation $E= MC^2$, but for his experiments proving something called the photo-electric effect. He demonstrated that when light strikes any material substance, electrons are discharged, creating an electric current. In other words, light interacts with matter. Colour is vibrating energy. As humans are electro-magnetic beings this would explain how the frequencies of light interact with our bodies.

If this is too abstract a concept consider how new-born infants with jaundice are routinely treated in hospital by shining a blue light on them. This helps to break down harmful levels of bilirubin in the skin.

Or how about this? Researchers at Cornell University Medical College in New York set out to test whether human circadian rhythms could be influenced by light that doesn't reach the eyes. They shone blue-green light - which quickly influences the sleep cycle - onto the backs of the subjects' knees for 3 hours. The result: Body core temperatures and melatonin outputs of the test subjects shifted consistently, in some cases by 3 hours.

You also shine the colour onto plain water – how does this turn the water into something that can help my arthritis, say?

Water is one of the most remarkable substances on earth. Because it is so plentiful we take it for granted. But, as a chemical substance, it is unique in at least 20 ways including the ability to retain the 'memory' of frequencies or patterns imprinted in it. So, after it is impregnated with the essential frequency your body currently needs, you can distribute this frequency throughout your physical system simply by drinking the water. Then your body takes what it requires to restore its balance and harmony and therefore its health.

135

That's the physical benefits but you also mentioned emotional, mental and spiritual – how do the frequencies of colours help in these areas?

Our physical bodies have an invisible counterpart, which extends beyond our skin, called the aura. This comprises different layers – the etheric, emotional, mental, astral and so on. Each vibrates at a different frequency and each relates to the emotional and mental states and spiritual attunement. These layers can be unbalanced by the many negative influences around us all the time. If any of them are disrupted, our health and well-being suffers. In a way yet to be understood, colours help to rebalance these layers and restore them to what you might call their 'factory setting'. This, in turn, rebalances, restores and revitalizes our whole system.

Which particular health issues does colour therapy help?

As far back as the 1920s Dr Kate Baldwin, a highly respected physician and chief surgeon of the Women's Hospital of Philadelphia, USA, was a strong proponent of colour therapy techniques both in her private practice, and within the hospital setting. She said at the time, 'After nearly 37 years of active hospital and private practice in medicine and surgery, I can produce quicker and more accurate results with colours than with any or all other methods combined—and with less strain on the patient.

'In many cases, the functions have been restored after the classical remedies have failed.   Sprains, bruises and traumata of all sorts respond to colour as to no other treatment. Septic conditions yield, regardless of the specific organism. Cardiac lesions, asthma, hay fever, pneumonia, inflammatory conditions of the eyes, corneal ulcers, glaucoma, and cataracts are relieved by the treatment.' In other words, there are very few conditions that Chromeopathy cannot help.

If it is such a miracle treatment, why doesn't every practice in every country use it today?

Sadly, the medical Establishment in the United States closed ranks against a therapy which seemed to threaten their recognised treatments and expertise. Practitioners were bullied and threatened with being struck off and colour therapy rapidly fell into disuse and was forgotten.

What is the situation in Europe?

The medical Establishment here did not actively oppose colour therapy. But when the era of antibiotics was ushered in after World War 2 the iron grip of the pharmaceutical industry began to take hold. The age of the clinical trial had arrived and treatments that could not be supported by 'scientific' fact were immediately suspect and walls were erected against complementary therapies like homoeopathy, naturopathy, and so on. However, light therapy is accepted by conventional medicine in some areas - particularly with the diagnosis of Seasonal Affective Disorder (SAD) and its treatment with light boxes. But the idea of individual colours having effects on organs is an acceptance too far.

If I choose to be treated by Intuitive Chromeopathy are there any side effects as there are sometimes with conventional drugs?

The treatment is all about the wavelengths and frequencies of our specially-selected colours which harmonise our organs and energy centres and balance any disrupted energy patterns. The result is reflected at all levels of our being – physical, emotional, mental and spiritual. The process is non-invasive and there are no side-effects. The only slightly unpleasant experience might be a temporary 'detox effect' which sometimes follows from bringing the system back into balance.

Take me through a typical session...how, for instance, would you treat me for persistant migraines?

After an initial chat explaining the concept behind Chromeopathy and some routine form-filling I would dowse or muscle-test the colour your system was in need of now to start you on the road to optimum health. Let's say we were guided to indigo, which is a combination of blue and violet. I would then dowse the radius of your aura, which is an indication of your current energy levels. Then I would set up the lamp with the indigo slide in front of the lens while you made yourself comfortable in the treatment chair. I would then switch on the beam which would be adjusted to shine on your head area, as well as on a bottle containing pure water.

As you relaxed I would lead you in a visualization exercise, breathing in the colour and distributing it to every atom and particle of your being. While you were in a relaxed state I would also balance your chakras with the pendulum. This whole process would take about half an hour. I would dowse your aura again to see how improved your energy levels are. After that I would decant the irradiated water into dispensers and prescribe two drops in a glass of water four times a day. This supplements the resonance your system needs until the next appointment.

What if I couldn't come back regularly because I was abroad? I have heard that remote consultations are possible. Is this correct?

Because we are dealing with subtle energy, also known as chi, prana, life force energy, cosmic energy etc., it works whatever the distance between practitioner and client. Modern science is now confirming the wisdom of the ancients and in particular quantum theory demonstrates the connectedness of everything through 'quantum entanglement' which Einstein referred to as 'spooky action at a distance.' So, yes, as time and space does not exist for the techniques used in Intuitive Chromeopathy, treatment can be delivered remotely.

When dealing with a client I lay out colour choices and muscle-test, or dowse, for which is needed. In colour therapy, when you bathe someone in a colour, it is quantumly-connected to all other colours of the same vibration and they are ALL brought to bear to heal. The body is a field of information and disease is a scrambling of this information. If you can correct the scrambling you can heal the disease.

The following is an extract from a scientific analysis of chromotherapy which brings in the concept of irradiating water: 'What was missing in their medicinal use of colour was water as a medium for the absorption of the colour, which later proved to be the best remedy for removing toxins from the body.'

That's a brief explanation of one modality, now let's get back to matters of the Mind and ways of focusing its power. One method is through the use of:

Hypnosis

This form of Mind control has been given a bad name by stage performers and is often thought, wrongly, to be a wacky practice. However, people can achieve superhuman feats under hypnosis, when all other thoughts are thrust aside and the Mind is concentrating on one objective.

Manifestations of such physical marvels were often demonstrated during the aforesaid stage performances when a volunteer from the audience would became as stiff as a board and would easily bear the weight of an adult sitting on his stomach while laid between two chairbacks, feet on one end and neck on the other. On the behavioural side, those in trances would cluck like chickens or jump up and down in excitement believing they had won the lottery.

But there's a serious point to all this for us. The volunteers' Minds had been pre-conditioned by *suggestion* which sets the scene for the power of BELIEF. What do I mean? Look at it this way: If the hypnotist was introduced, even before appearing on stage, as a famous mesmerist who has honed his powers under the guidance of a mysterious sect of Buddhist monks, it's odds-on that 90% of the audience would become susceptible to his charms.

But if he was announced as a long-distance lorry driver and part-time actor, who was going to pretend to be a hypnotist, then his task would be nigh-on impossible. The foundation of success here is BELIEF. It's that ability to BELIEVE that makes the Mind so powerful when it comes to changing your life. But, steer clear of stage hypnotists and learn how to self-hypnotise to achieve amazing things.

Emotional Freedom Technique

BELIEF is crucial to successful outcomes. A placebo works because of BELIEF. Another example of a healing protocol that appears to work miracles is the non-invasive EFT, or Emotional Freedom Technique, which clearly owes its success to the clients BELIEF. EFT is a practical, self-help method that involves using the fingers to gently tap on the body's acupuncture points along the meridian lines of Chinese medicine.

It is often referred to as simply 'Tapping'. The therapeutic effects of this technique are recognized around the world. People use it for anxiety, weight loss issues, pain, stress and many other health problems. Father of the technique is Gary Craig who is still developing his methods, healing an increasing range of physical, emotional, mental and spiritual issues. He has even started teaching it to practitioners to treat serious illnesses.

Gary tells his students: 'We make the assumption that one of the major causes, if not THE major cause of all serious diseases, is a disruption in the body's energy system and/or unresolved emotional issues. Clearly, there can be other causes, such as diet and lifestyle, but in my experience the emotional contributors to these ailments are far larger than most people think.'

So, how can just tapping on the body's acupuncture points treat, and often cure, serious conditions? BELIEF is a big part of the therapy. While the practitioner taps, or the patient self-taps, the unconscious Mind goes to work clearing out all the emotional contributors to the illness, disease, phobia, allergy, or whatever. The result can often seem miraculous. But the power of the Mind knows no bounds.

In some mysterious way our Minds connect to the Infinite Mind (some might say the Akashic Record) and work their wonders sometimes without us even being aware of it. An example of this is something that occurred during the career of one of the UK's greatest spiritual healers, Harry Edwards. Harry, a printer by trade, discovered his healing gifts during his service as a Captain in the Royal Sussex Regiment during the First World War. He was sent to Persia (now Iran) to take charge of scores of local labourers who were tasked with building a link between two sections of the Baghdad to Mosul Railway.

Injuries and illness led to many of the locals coming to him for medical treatment, despite the fact that Harry had only the barest essentials with which to treat them. Nevertheless, the recovery rate was remarkable and word soon spread of his healing powers. After the war Harry joined a spiritualist group and was encouraged to intercede on behalf of a person dying from tuberculosis, who subsequently made an excellent recovery. His next patient had been diagnosed with terminal cancer who, following Harry Edwards' help, soon became well enough to return to work.

Many similar cases followed and, as media interest increased, Harry's reputation - and that of Spiritual Healing in general - soared. Harry's healing work now became a major part of his life.

At the height of his ministry he was receiving over 10,000 letters a week. In 1948 he conducted a healing demonstration in Manchester attended by 6,000 people. This was only one of many similar gatherings conducted in venues from Newcastle to Amsterdam. At each one he would roll up his sleeves and, with his characteristic humour and humility, bring healing to people of all ages and backgrounds.

Distant healing was a major part of his work and he, assisted now by a large support team, meticulously kept the names and medical needs of thousands writing in begging for on-going intercession. Harry would send his healing vibrations remotely to all those on file. Then, disaster struck. A catastrophic fire destroyed all the records and all the daily prayers for individuals ceased.

Harry was devastated. He was going to let down all those desperate folk who had put their trust in him and who needed his healing powers. But to his astonishment he continued to receive thank you letters from hundreds of people who, apparently, were still being healed and were often enjoying miraculous recoveries. How could this be? Thought Harry. How could sick people in such large numbers be cured when he didn't even know who they were? Answer: BELIEF.

He may not have known them, but the Universe knew them so Harry's healing prayers were delivered to those in need. And, of course, while Harry might not have known each sufferer personally, they all knew him and knew he would be sending out his healing thoughts to them every day. So their BELIEF was the healer. At the risk of being tedious this is 100 per cent relevant...BELIEF is the miracle-worker. BELIEF makes it happen. Dissociative Identity Disorder sufferers can change from blue-eyed to brown-eyed, or recover instantly from a duodenal ulcer because they BELIEVE they are different people. Placebo effect (belief) is paramount...Thus, people will be healed by homeopathy, or a radionics machine, or colour therapy because of BELIEF. But, is it the belief of the practitioner or patient or both?

In his book *The Energy Cure* healer Bill Bengston comes to the conclusion that trying to heal didn't work. What he did was 'carry in my Mind the desired intent for a healing outcome while not consciously concerning myself about how it might occur.' So, does he hand the details over to the Infinite Mind to get on with the job? Like what seemed to have happened with Harry Edwards? Bengston found that the healing process was triggered by the biological needs of the organism being treated (the need reaching out for the cure?). Again, shades of Harry Edwards's supplicants here. However, we might theorise that Bill Bengston's healing protocol and Harry Edwards's prayers were being actively sought by the need.

An astonishing experiment carried out by Bengston seems to support this idea. He engaged 'healers' to hold healing intent in their Minds while a machine dropped unmarked envelopes, containing details of sick animals, into their hands. The participants had no idea what the animals, or their conditions, were. All they needed to do was hold healing intent in their hearts. The experiment, carried out with strict protocols, resulted in the animals' health improving. The implication here being - similar to Harry Edwards's experience – as long as the healing intent was sincere somehow the need reached out for the cure and was 'connected' to it.

Curiously Bengston found, similar to William Tiller, that he could 'charge' secondary substances – like cotton, wood shavings and water - with healing power.

But, is it all much simpler than this? Are we all just following that Master Plan we discussed earlier? Rather than the cure seeking the need, or the need seeking the cure, the healing is just part of the cosmic drama we're all caught up in where we play our parts to achieve a pre-ordained outcome?

In Hazel Courteney's book *Countdown to Coherence* she quotes stock market trader-turned author Gary Renard, who claims to have conversed with two 'angels' Arten and Pursah. They told him everything is predestined with multiple alternative endings. Although you can't change the script you can change how you deal with events and that's what is important. 'We may not have a choice as to what we experience but we always have a choice how we experience it.'

Another thought to ponder: When any healers – homeopath, radionics specialist, colour therapist, reiki master etc go through their procedures, it is not the procedures that work but the INTENT allied to BELIEF behind them. That is why dowser David Cowen can chisel a line on a stone, place the stone on a detrimental energy ley and divert that line to a harmless trajectory...The stone contains David's INTENT which continues to exist long after David is dead! Ditto the homeopath's water, the radionics rate and the colour therapist's colours. Our Minds have the power to create an outcome and that power can remain for ever.

The first point I would make about some of what I'm reading is that it contains such a head-spinning collection of theories, mixed in with healing modalities and therapies, it's difficult to grasp what I'm supposed to take away. For instance, should I be pondering on the relative efficacy of healing modalities? Or should I be more impressed by the power of belief and intent? Or would I be better served by thinking about the Many Worlds Theory and how it affects my mortal soul?

I think whatever jumps out at you is what the Universe knows you need at this time. My role in writing this book has been not so much as an author but more a channeler – writing what I'm told. It's the Universe's way of getting info out to those who need it. While Harry Edwards's healing went where it was needed the contents of this book will find its intended target. And, by the way, my purpose is not to give you all the answers but to stimulate your Mind to find its own. You may come up with a profound truth that I would never think of just by putting the right pieces of the jigsaw together.

OK I've re-read some recent bits and what jumped out at me was David Hawkins's notion that the human Mind is like a computer terminal connected to a giant database, which is mankind's common consciousness. And that he can tap into it by pressing on someone's arm. I know this concept could be important to me but it all sounds like more hocus-pocus and not really relevant to my world.

Dr Hawkins (who died in 2012 at the age of 85) had a global following and has dramatically changed many people's lives. He had taken some universal truths and made them his own in his own style. Fifty years before him Carl Gustav Jung, a Swiss psychiatrist and psychoanalyst, who founded analytical psychology, became famous for his theory of humankind's 'Collective Unconscious.' This, he claimed, was the part of the Mind that contains memories and ideas inherited from our ancestors. You could equate this with the wider concept of the Akashic Record which, as we've already touched on, is a sort of Cosmic database of all knowledge.

That I'm sort of OK with. It's the idea that pressing on someone's arm gives you unlimited access to this database that I find difficult to accept. Has Hawkins ever proved any of this stuff?

You can easily see for yourself if what he claims is true. _Power Vs. Force_ is readily available, even in many local libraries, and testing his method will only take a few minutes.

That sounds like a cop-out to me. I have to buy another book to find out if something in yours might or might not be valid.

Sorry if you think I'm being evasive. All I'm trying to do is point you to a source of information which will cover in great detail something I can only touch on here.

Alright, I've got another question. The idea of non-invasive colour therapy sounds ideal. But, again, is there any actual evidence that it works in the real world?

You're going to hate me for this, but I'm going to recommend another book! It's called _Light Therapies – A Complete Guide to the Healing Power of Light_ by physicist and electronics designer Anadi Martel. The info in it is backed by 30 years of research and covers pretty well every modality using colour and light to heal – in particular the interaction between light, biology, and consciousness. And just in case you're wondering – No, my Intuitive Chromeopathy is not included in the book.

Again, you haven't answered my question: Is there any real evidence that it works in the real world?

That's what I'm trying to tell you, Anadi Martel's book is full of examples – from cancer and Alzheimer's to skin diseases and heart problems - enough to convince even the most died-in-the-wool sceptic.

The Mind of man is capable of anything - Joseph Conrad

13 THE DAY FRANCESCA TALKED WITH A NAIL

When Leslie Lemke was born prematurely, he had brain damage, cerebral palsy, and had to have his eyes surgically removed due to glaucoma. When he was put up for adoption aged six months, May, a nurse who was 52 with 5 children of her own, welcomed him into her family.

When Leslie was 16, May was woken up in the middle of the night by the sound of a piano playing in her downstairs sitting room. Thinking she'd left the television on she went downstairs to turn it off. When she entered the room she was astonished to find Leslie playing Tchaikovsky's Piano Concerto No. 1 flawlessly on their baby grand – he had heard it on TV earlier that day.

From that day on, despite him having no musical training, Leslie began to play all styles of music - from ragtime to classical. All it took for him to play a composition perfectly was to hear the music once. For many years afterwards, before his health declined, he gave regular concerts in the US, Japan and Scandinavia, and also appeared on many US TV shows.

Another astonishing person is Ellen, who has stunned the world with her ability as a human chronometer. When she was eight Ellen became fascinated by the speaking clock, listening to every announcement, right down to every last second. From then on Ellen was able to tell the exact time - precisely to each hour, minute, and second of the day.

Similar to Leslie, Ellen also has exceptional musical talents and can play compositions perfectly after hearing them just once. Famously, a reporter once tried to catch her out by asking her to reproduce obscure songs, but Ellen played every one.

Both Leslie and Ellen are Savants. This is a human condition brought to the world's attention by the fictional character Raymond Babbitt, played by Dustin Hoffman, in the 1988 film 'Rain Man.' Savant syndrome is a rare, but extraordinary, condition in which people with serious mental disabilities, including autism, have an individual genius which stands in marked contrast to their disability. Whatever the particular savant skill, it is always linked to massive memory.

The real 'Rain Man' was Kim Peek. What Kim could do was astounding: he had read some 12,000 books and remembered everything about them. 'Kimputer,' as he was lovingly known to many, used to read two pages at once - his left eye scannng the left page while his right eye read the right page. It took him about 3 seconds to get through two pages. Kim could recall facts and trivia from 15 subject areas from history to geography to sports. Tell him a date, and Kim could tell you what day of the week it was. He also remembered all the music he had ever heard.

Some savants are also known as Lightning Calculators. These are people who can do mental arithmetic very fast in their heads without using a pencil, paper or a calculator. Daniel Tammet first became famous when he recited Pi from memory to 22,514 decimal places - a feat which took over 5 hours.

Numbers, according to Daniel, are special to him. He actually 'sees' figures and calculations – a rare ability called synaesthesia. In his Mind each number from 1 to 10,000 has its own unique shape, colour, texture and feel. He has described 289 as being particularly ugly, 333 as especially attractive, and Pi as beautiful.

Besides those who are born savants, there are also people who are 'acquired savants' – who gain a new, extraordinary ability after a stroke, brain injury, or dementia.

So once again the ability of the Mind to tap into a field of information 'out there' is dramatically demonstrated. But is there any way that ordinary mortals like you and me can access this information? The answer is a definite 'Yes.' One of the ways that ordinary folk become extraordinary is through the ancient skill of Dowsing.

The word 'dowsing' falls far short of encapsulating the Mind-boggling possibilities which it offers. I've tried to find other, more appropriate words but there just aren't any. In France they call it radiesthesia. It's a bit like we still use the word 'broadcasting' to describe sending a radio signal from transmitter to receiver. But the word doesn't distinguish between the ordinary and the extraordinary. It could mean anything from a crude walkie-talkie with a range of 10 metres to a satellite 24,000 miles above our heads transmitting a high definition, three dimensional, colour television picture to a 70 inch LED flat screen TV.

In computer terms, dowsing is a kind of spiritual search engine – scanning all that is known for answers to anything and everything: From, 'Will this melon be ripe in time for my dinner party on Wednesday?' To, 'How many past lives have I lived?' From, 'Should I wear a waterproof coat today?' To, 'Why is my relationship not working?' Dowsing for answers is limited only by your imagination. And it is the key to the supernatural potential I deal with in *Dowse Your Way To Psychic Power*.

Any of the following words could justifiably be used in connection with aspects of this ancient art...mysterious, supernatural, paranormal, mystical, psychic, clairvoyant, uncanny, bizarre, mumbo-jumbo, weird. Dowsing creates a bridge between two worlds – those of the visible and the invisible. Dowsers will tell you the practice answers questions that are beyond the scope of our normal five senses.

A recent study by scientists tested the depth of meditation reached by adepts like yogis, Sufis, and monks. This was done by measuring their brainwave patterns. The scientists discovered that professional dowsers reached the same Theta levels as Zen Buddhists, who had perfected their techniques over many years.

In short, dowsing harnesses the ability still there deep down in each one of us – our Intuition. And through honing our intuition, we become increasingly psychic. So what exactly is Dowsing and how can you learn its ancient skills? Here's a quick Q&A on the subject which you may find helpful:

What is dowsing?

It is the ancient art, in growing use today, of seeking information not available to our five senses - from locating underground water and minerals, tracing lost pets & people, to diagnosing allergies, choosing therapies or improving the well being of our living environment.

Is dowsing a special gift?

No, almost everyone can dowse. It's rather like riding a bike or learning a musical instrument - some are gifted but for the rest of us practise, practise, practise makes perfect.

What tools do you use?

The primary instrument is the Mind of the dowser. To engage the Mind in the dowsing process the dowser uses any of four main tools - the pendulum, the Y-rod (forked stick), the L-rod or the bobber. These act as indicators much as a needle on a gauge. The tools respond in a binary fashion giving yes/no or true/false answers to carefully worded questions (rather like the muscle-testing we've already talked about. In fact, muscle-testing is a form of dowsing). Dowsing is sometimes called 'divining' indicating that the source of the answers might be from a higher consciousness or the Infinite Mind.

How does it work?

Nobody really knows. There is a consensus emerging that when our Minds receive the answers to the question our muscles respond and this response is magnified by the dowsing tool we are using. There is no magic in the pendulum or rod - if there is any magic at all it is in us.

What is dowsing used for in the 21st Century?

The more the digital age dominates our lives the less we are feeling connected to the world of nature around us. The dowsing instrument gives us back that connectedness with the Universe in both a practical and spiritual way. On the one hand dowsing can be used for locating minerals, water, archaeological remains or lost objects; on the other it can detect unseen energies, both natural and man-made, some of which are harmful to our health. Many dowsers use the process to test the nutritional value of food, diagnose physical ailments, plan gardens, or study ancient sacred sites like Stonehenge.

How can a person get started?

Joining a dowsing group would be a good way as you can be guided in the techniques by others who have walked the path before you. However, that is not essential. The first three steps are: find a tool that suits you, get your Mind ready, and assume the ready position. You don't need to buy expensive devices from the internet as they are easy to make at home - a wire coat hanger can be fashioned into a pair of L-rods and a key on a piece of thread will work as a pendulum. The internet is full of 'how to ' information. Or there are plenty of inexpensive books on dowsing available.

Could I make a paid career of dowsing?

Some do, ranging from multi-millionaire specialists hired by oil or mining companies to the more humble health practitioner who is happy to earn a living doing what he/she loves. For most, though, it is a fascinating hobby which can transform your life.

Dowsing is like that theoretical wormhole in space that connects far away places - it enables you to jump straight there without the tedious business of travelling thousands of light years and waiting several lifetimes. Dowsing is a bridge to that 'information field' - or the Akashic Record - which contains everything you will ever need to know.

On your dowsing journey you may travel through territory containing the mystical and the paranormal. By the time you reach your destination you could have encountered angels, spirit guides, elementals, ghosts, poltergeists and entities that dwell in other dimensions. You will have been introduced to precognition, retro-cognition, trance states, possession, past lives and re-incarnation.

You will know how to communicate with animals and plants, how to move energy from one place to another and how to go back, and forward, in time. Along the way you will learn what paranormal skills are available to you and which are the ones that will make you a unique 'psychic.'

Having tuned your Mind, through dowsing, to the psychic dimension you'll be encountering our now familiar Alice in Wonderland world occupied by the Quantum physicists where weird things happen that break the rules of conventional science.

Let's recap on our journey in this book so far and apply dowsing to this realm: We could ask, Do poltergeists have a Mind? What about angels? Are those suffering from Dissociative Identity Disorder actually possessed by the Minds of dead people? Do the Minds of those having an Out-of-Body experience still function while the brain is switched off? Will there ever be a 'rational' explanation for psychic and Quantum anomalous phenomena? And do inanimate objects have some form of consciousness?

I look at many of these conundrums in my book *In Tune With The Infinite Mind,* but as we're dealing specifically with Mind Power here let's look at cases where some kind of intelligence appears to be at work. In *The Psychic Investigator's Casebook* Archibald Lawrie tells some startling stories.   Working with an experienced medium called Francesca he's encountered a child poltergeist who's showered them with hundreds of smarties, which dropped on their heads out of nowhere; they've witnessed a meeting between Mary Queen of Scots and her lover, the Earl of Bothwell in 1566. And have had mental conversations with a nail.

Yes, you read that correctly, Francesca talked with a nail. She tuned into its 'consciousness' and it told her that it had been used in building a ship. But now the ship had been decommissioned, the nail had been re-assigned and it was sad. Which brings us to:

Panpsychism

Conversations with a nail might seem odd, but not if you accept the notion of panpsychism. This is the theory that everything has a consciousness, not just sentient beings. That's why some people, particularly dowsers, dialogue with megaliths and sacred sites.   Panpsychists believe that consciousness permeates all physical matter. And that things know your thoughts and how you feel about them.

It is difficult to believe in panpsychism because it is highly counterintuitive. How can a nail have an inner life? But are not many widely accepted scientific theories counter to common sense? Albert Einstein says time slows down at high speeds. And, according to Charles Darwin's theory of evolution, our ancestors were apes. All of these views are wildly at odds with our common-sense view of the world, or at least they were when they were first proposed. Panpsychism seeks to unite the Universe as one overall, grand consciousness.

After all, isn't it logical that, if the entire universe resulted from a primordial Big Bang, then everything in it shares the same fundamental components, like atoms. And atoms comprise even smaller parts like protons, neutrons and electrons. And these, in turn, are made up of quarks. We humans, and everything around us, and throughout the Cosmos, are made of the same stuff. And all that stuff has its own consciousness.

Defining consciousness has eluded the best brains on the planet so the 'panpsychist' view is increasingly being embraced by reputable philosophers, scientists, and physicists, including people like neuroscientist Christof Koch and physicist Roger Penrose. British physicist, astronomer and mathematician Sir James Jeans waded into the debate when he said, 'The Universe looks more and more like a great thought rather than a great machine. Mind is the creator and governor of this realm.'

So, while no-one is suggesting megaliths will one day get together and take over the world, they do have a rudimentary 'Mind' as do trees, houses, machines or locations. In fact we are interconnected with everything in the Universe which is why, (forgive the pun) if we put our Minds to it, we can communicate with selected parts of it. And, instinctively, deep down, we buy into this theory. Not convinced? How often has your car not started and you've pleaded with it not to let you down? Or, when the weather has seemed to be deliberately trying to thwart your plans for a family barbecue you've exhorted it to give you a break?

Some scientific big hitters are now embracing the idea that everything has a consciousness. German-British philosopher F C S Schiller says, 'A stone, no doubt, does not apprehend us as spiritual beings... But does this amount to saying that it does not apprehend us at all, and takes no note whatever of our existence? Not at all; it is aware of us and affected by us on the plane on which its own existence is passed... It faithfully exercises all of its physical functions, and influences us by so doing. It gravitates and resists pressure, and obstructs...vibrations, and so forth, and makes itself respected as such a body. And it treats us as if of a like nature with itself, on the level of its understanding...'

Polymath, physicist, biologist, biophysicist, botanist and archaeologist, Sir Jagadish Chandra Bose, one of the most prominent Indian scientists, proved by experimentation that both animals and plants shared much in common. He demonstrated that plants are also sensitive to heat, cold, light, noise and various other external stimuli. He caused a stir in his scientific community when he added that inanimate objects had the same responses too. He said famously, 'I have studied metals all my career and I am happy to think that they have life.'

The aforementioned dowsers love stone circles and have a method of dialoguing with them. This is how they are advised to prepare before divining at a sacred/megalithic site:

'Quieten your rational Mind - if you try to make sense of dialoguing with the stones, you won't.

'Tune in to the consciousness of the stones and allow it to interact with yours.

'Be aware (but don't analyse) how you feel on an emotional level. Then, as you move about the site, ask whatever questions you feel appropriate – eg When was the site built? What was its purpose - Religious? Ceremonial? Astronomical? Other?

'Do the stones retain their power?

164

'Does water run beneath the site? Does this feed the site's energies?

'Do energy lines run through and around the site?

'Do the stones communicate with others in the area?

'Can the stones help me? Can I help them?

'Is there a special spot for me to stand today?

'Is there a special stone ready to feed its energy to me today?

'What message are the stones communicating to me today?

'Do the stones have a healing purpose?

'Do I have a healing purpose?

'Is there any else of interest to me to find? If so show me where.

'Finally, remember to protect yourself before entering the site.'

There's someone in my head, but it's not me - Pink Floyd

14 I'M UNDER ATTACK! (OR AM I JUST TIRED?)

Protect yourself? What are the dowsers being exhorted to protect themselves against? Well, for a start something called spirit attachment is very real. Spiritual gurus down the ages have contended that we are surrounded by entities that we cannot see but are real in their own dimensions. Often these discarnate energies cluster around sacred sites, possibly brought there by human visitors, and will seek a new body to inhabit.

Since science maintains energy cannot be destroyed, it can only change form, it seems logical that extreme emotions like hate, fear, love etc send out their own vibrations which, like a charge of electricity, find a haven with other, like energies. So, in our daily lives we feed these energies and entities, who can then return to us to help or harm us.

In fact our world seems to be the natural habitat of negative entities, which defy any known system of reference. Their logic dominates the material world of politics and commerce, in which man's inhumanity to man is a familiar experience - where tyranny prospers and evil empires flourish.

Lurking out of the visible spectrum are populations of these unseen beings who take the form of whatever the Mind desires. They are 'tuning in' to the myriad energies that abound in the Universe, including those we humans have created, and they feed on them to sustain their forms. They are active and intelligent and are able to act physically on people in the same way as people act physically on each other.

There are a lot of low spirits abounding in the Universes next door awaiting opportunities to partake, second-hand, of the old lusts and thrills of earthly life. Some are activated by malice, others merely mischievous, but they draw their energies from their hosts, or whatever is available in the invisible realm. Low moral ideals (low vibrations) attract these low spirits while high ideals (high vibrations) do the opposite.

Perhaps we are all possessed in one way or another. Some believe common-or-garden thoughts are intelligent entities that 'possess' the human form and use us to carry out their purpose. When we decide to go shopping, or stay at home, or do some deadheading in the garden, is it 'us' having these thoughts or is it our possessing entity that is pulling our strings for its own ends? In fact who ARE we? Are we our bodies? Our Minds? Is there just one version of us?

Are most of us inhabited by several thought entities at the same time who are often at war within us, changing our personalities as we react to events? When Mozart said, 'Tunes just walk into my head' perhaps he was right - his Mind acting as a receptacle for music dropping from the spheres. Thoughts are no different. Mozart was a genius because his thoughts were geniuses. Some of us are idiots because that's the way our thoughts take us.

Is it possible that 'out there' is a jungle of competing thoughts swirling around in their own dimension until they burst through into ours seeking a life within the vehicle of our bodies? When our bodies die do our thoughts, who inhabited us, merely re-enter their own dimension and wait for another suitable vehicle within which to continue their existence. Do we have thoughts, or do thoughts have us? Now there's a thought.

Symptoms of Psychic Attacks and Dark Energies

If the entire universe is made of the same stuff and if this stuff shares an overall consciousness, everything in it is connected and intermingling, separated only by the frequency in which it lives and has its being. As I said, among the inhabitants who share our universe are dark forces who, like bacteria or viruses, seek to infect human existence.

But, just like a viral or bacterial infection, which make their presence known through disease and illness, there are many different symptoms that can indicate negative psychic energies, spirits or entities inhabiting our being. The following list identifies a few major pointers. But these symptoms can also indicate other types of health problems so, before you suspect psychic attack, it's important to investigate all possibilities. But here are the signs to look out for:

- Suddenly acting totally out of character

- Other major changes in behaviour for no reason

- A loss of memory

- Major changes in clarity of thinking or analytical ability

- Sudden ongoing fatigue for no apparent reason

- A drained feeling

ANTHONY TALMAGE

- Icy cold sensation on part or all of your body

- Hearing someone's voice in your head regularly

- Hearing voices generally

- Recurrent or frequent nightmares

- Strange or recurring accidents

- Feeling someone is watching you

- A discomfort or fear in a specific room or area in your home or office

- A drastic loss of self-confidence

- A sudden loss of energy

- An illness that eludes diagnosis

- Feeling someone touch you or bump into you when nobody is present

- Sensing a presence

- Sensing a large pair of eyes watching you or following you

- Sudden or irrational difficulties with finances or relationships

170

- Imagining monsters, animals or frightening shadows

- Seeming ongoing bad luck

- Visions or hallucinations

- Irrational fear, anger or sorrow

- A negative obsessive thought, desire or fetish that won't go away

The 'spirits' are drawn to people by their vibrations - if these people are depressed, or at a low ebb, they attract 'lower' vibrations which exist in a 'cloud' of bundled holographic frequencies. A part of the cloud is attracted to the human being and lodges in his/her energy field and takes on a life of its own. This life then develops by reacting to the environment of the host as well as drawing on a 'collective memory' from the cloud.

Then the attachment becomes stronger and more dominant and, depending on the demeanour of the part of the cloud it is connected to, develops in a negative way - thus negatively affecting its host. It is not a 'spirit' that has lived before, rather a composite of earth bound intelligencies which either have a negative or positive motivation. The negatively-motivated composites reinforce the negativity of their hosts which feeds back into the cloud.

Meanwhile, the earthly life of the host is dragged lower and lower. This extreme situation is rare so let's continue on a more positive note and get back to 'out there' where there's an 'information field' accessible by savants, dowsers, mediums and psychics – and us! A reminder: this is our equivalent of the Akashic Record, believed in by Buddhists, occultists and adherents of the Theosophy religion, who claim that data on everything that has ever happened, is happening or will happen is imprinted on the basic structure of the entire universe.

This means that everything you think, feel, say or do is recorded and stored in perpetuity. A memory card contains a recording of an event. The Akashic Record is similar but with added smells, tastes, colours and even thoughts and emotions. The 'Akasha,' or 'Astral Light,' is believed by Theosophists to be accessible by persons such as clairvoyants or spiritual beings. They do this by using their 'astral bodies' or 'astral senses' to gain access to these stored spiritual insights

A remarkable Mind that seemed able to access information from the Akashic Record was someone who became the best-known psychic in the world. He was American mystic Edgar Cayce, who died in 1945. He was known as the 'Sleeping Prophet,' the 'father of holistic medicine,' and he was the most documented psychic of the 20th century. Cayce was born on a farm in Hopkinsville, Kentucky, in 1877, and his psychic abilities began to appear as early as his childhood.

As an adult, Cayce would put himself into a state of meditation, connect with the Universal Consciousness, and from this state came his 'readings'. From holistic health and the treatment of illness to dream interpretation and reincarnation, Cayce's readings and insights offered practical help and advice to thousands of individuals from all walks of life.

When 'patients' went to his consulting room Cayce would lie on his couch and go to sleep. While apparently unconscious he would dictate his diagnosis, sometimes using medical terms he had no knowledge of in his waking state. His patients were often completely cured.

The repeated accuracy of his diagnoses and the effectiveness of the sometimes unorthodox treatments he prescribed made him a medical phenomenon. His patients did not even need to be physically present for him to work his magic. He needed only the name and current location of an individual anywhere in the world to give a diagnosis. Eventually the scope of his work expanded to include information and advice on thousands of subjects, including mental and spiritual counsel, metaphysics, parapsychology, religion, and prophecy of personal and world events.

These days there are sensitives who work as Akashic Record Consultants. One such is Alison King, who tunes in to specific places in the energy matrix that human beings create with their thoughts, feelings and actions. So she will experience the feelings of the person who created that part of the matrix and will be able to describe those feelings to the enquirer.

How does it work? In the realms of metaphysical or unseen energy, there is no such thing as time, space or matter as we understand it in the material world. So, following the logic of this, Alison can just as easily tune in to someone who has been dead for nearly a thousand years as to someone who had lived relatively recently. Alison has turned this ability into a practical collaboration. Back in 2004 her author friend, Elizabeth Chadwick, was having difficulties researching one of her characters, a medieval mistress, who had actually lived. So Alison offered to 'tune in' to the character.

She was so successful in filling in the gaps that Elizabeth asked her to work with her on a regular basis. Alison says, 'To date, I have provided Akashic research for Elizabeth's novels *The Greatest Knight, The Scarlet Lion, A Place Beyond Courage, The Time of Singing, To Defy a King, Lady of the*

English, The Summer Queen, The Winter Crown and The Autumn Throne.'

As a result the pair have amassed an enormous amount of material - hundreds of thousands of words - on all aspects of medieval life.

Another example of tapping into information floating about in the ether is the art of Psychometry. This is again sensing the energy of matter - this time by reading objects by touch. Psychometry generally refers to the ability to gain impressions and information about an object, or anything connected to it, by holding it in your hand. A person with this ability is called a Psychometrist or a Scryer.

The term was coined in 1842 by Joseph R Buchanan, an American physiologist, who claimed it could be used to measure the 'soul' of all things. Buchanan further said that the past is entombed in the present. Archibald Lawrie, mentioned earlier, has come up with a unique theory about psychometry. The object, he said, does not in itself contain the information, like a memory stick. Rather, the object acts as a transmitter/receiver connecting the sensitive to information stored in the Akashic Record.

As we now know, the ancient art of dowsing can tap into this record, too. Using the power of the pendulum, diviners

175

work outside the realms of time and space with their Yes/No questions: What colour eyes did Cleopatra have – blue? No; brown? No; Green? Yes. Did Henry VIII really love any of his wives? Yes. Was it Catherine of Aragon? No; Anne Boleyn? No…you get the idea. In effect dowsers do what Alison King does.

I have lots of questions about things in these last two chapters. For a start, has anyone ever come up with a theory as to how these savants do what they do?

The conventional explanation is that savant-ism is caused by damage to the left hemisphere of the brain combined with a phenomenal memory. This allows the right (intuitive) brain to tap into a hidden reservoir which we all have but which we rarely access.

However, this sounds to me typical of the contortions scientists go to just to avoid admitting there might be a mysterious something outside of ourselves that creates the phenomenon. As it cannot be analysed in a laboratory it therefore does not exist. So the academics fall back on half-baked theories that actually don't add up. OK, damage to the left brain is perfectly logical but to then suggest that somehow that allows access to a reservoir of information hidden deep down is illogical. For a start, where does that information come from?

I could argue the case for the scientists, but I suspect we'd never agree so let's move on to Panpsychism. The idea that all matter has some form of consciousness sounds plain loopy. It's just another theory. Where's the proof?

That's a bit like saying prove that God exists. All we can do is say that for a lot of people panpsychism makes perfect sense. Phillip Goff is associate professor in philosophy at the Central European University in Budapest. And his research interest is in consciousness. Writing in Aeon Magazine he says the theory of panpsychism is crazy but most probably true. He says, 'I maintain that there is a powerful simplicity argument in favour of panpsychism. The argument relies on a claim that has been defended by Bertrand Russell, Arthur Eddington and many others, namely that physical science doesn't tell us what matter *is*, only what it *does*.'

He goes on, 'In the public mind, physics is on its way to giving us a complete picture of the nature of space, time and matter. While in this mindset, panpsychism seems improbable, as physics does not attribute experience to fundamental particles. But once we realise that physics tells us nothing about the intrinsic nature of the entities it talks about...the issue looks very different.

'All we get from physics is this big black-and-white abstract structure, which we must somehow colour in with

177

intrinsic nature. We know how to colour in one bit of it: the brains of organisms are coloured in with experience. How to colour in the rest? The most elegant, simple, sensible option is to colour in the rest of the world with the same pen.

'Panpsychism is crazy. But it is also highly likely to be true.'

That's just one so-called expert's opinion. It doesn't go anywhere near providing a convincing case. I repeat, where's the proof?

There's no actual proof that would stand up in a court of law. But then neither is there to support the Big Bang theory which most scientists now accept as a viable idea as to how the Universe began. However, another supporter of panpsychism is our friend biologist Rupert Sheldrake, who puts forward a convincing argument in his book *Science Set Free.*

In it he says, 'Panpsychism is not a new idea. Most people used to believe in it, and many still do. All over the world, traditional people saw the world around them as alive and in some sense conscious or aware: the planets, stars, the earth, plants and animals all had spirits or souls. Ancient Greek philosophy grew up in this context. In medieval Europe, philosophers and theologians took for granted that the world was full of animate beings. Plants and animals had souls, and stars and planets were governed by intelligences.

'Panpsychism raises all sorts of new questions. As the materialist worldview loses its grip, we can begin to think about human and nonhuman minds in new ways.'

I think that question's run its course. Let's move on to so-called possession. Are you really saying that in the 21st Century - the age of computers and Artificial Intelligence – some people are still stuck in medieval times and talk about evil spirits and being possessed?

Despite humankind's advances in technology, human nature has not changed in 50,000 years since we developed from Neanderthals. And neither have the primordial fears of the spirit world.

Our fears might not have changed but my point is those fears are demonstrated by the modern world to be irrational and irrelevant.

Ah, if only that were so. The human race is as much under attack from dark forces as it ever was. If readers of *In Tune With The Infinite Mind* will forgive me I could give you a real-life example, which I quoted in the book, of a kind of possession which was actually quite benign, but it illustrates how vulnerable we all are to being '"taken over" by some kind of intelligence.

It is the case of award-winning journalist Hazel Courteney. When she popped into Harrods on April 8 1998 to buy some Easter eggs something happened which changed her life. As she made her way through the turnstile to the bread hall it stuck fast – it wouldn't go forward, it wouldn't go back. As Hazel was deciding her next move…well, let her take up the story in her own words… 'I felt a searing bolt of – of something – coursing through my body. I can only describe it as "energy." The pain in my chest was appalling. I could hear a voice, not my own but inside my head, shouting "See a doctor – now."

Hazel says that voice, which possibly saved her life, was that of Diana, Princess of Wales who, by that time, had been dead for seven months. Suddenly the turnstile moved and Hazel stumbled towards the exit and found a telephone to call her doctor who, after tests, found no heart problems but diagnosed a severe panic attack. Later that night while lying in bed pondering on the events of the day, the voice returned. It kept repeating, 'I have died and come back.' Hazel, a perfectly normal and balanced busy wife and mother, had never experienced anything psychic or paranormal. This episode was totally alien to her down-to-earth approach to life, and subsequent events completely changed her view on discarnate intelligencies. She went on to write a book about her experience called *Divine Intervention.*

That seems very weird – but a story with a happy ending. Going back to the so-called possessions that are more malign. Tell me how they happen. Who's being attacked? Where's the evidence?

I suggest you read psychologist Dr Edith Fiore's book *The Unquiet Dead.* If that doesn't convince you nothing will. I mention her book because it summarises where the human race seems to be in the 21st Century when it comes to 'entities.' As a professional she deals with modern cases of spirit attack and possession.

How about some real life examples – but from someone other than Dr Fiore?

OK. Let's look at the experiences of psychiatrist Dr Alan Sanderson who, believe it or not, used to conduct spirit release therapy for the UK's National Health Service. In a paper for the Royal College of Psychiatrists he contends that spirit attachment is 'a common and an eminently treatable phenomenon.' He writes that throughout his 50 years as a medic the psychiatric profession's understanding of the nature and causes of emotional disorder 'has advanced scarcely at all.'

He says, 'The problems posed by people cutting themselves, abusing drugs and alcohol, suffering periods of depression or experiencing bizarre thoughts and behaviour, seem as great as ever, and we remain in almost total ignorance of the underlying causes. The biological approach, which a century ago appeared to hold out such hope for psychiatry, has run out of steam.'

He adds, 'Yet, because this remains the only scientifically "respectable" approach, nothing new is being tried.' So he decided to train in spirit release therapy and subsequently treated hundreds of patients 'and I can say that spirit attachment, as it is now called, is a common condition for which, in many cases, there is an effective and safe treatment.'

By way of illustration Dr Sanderson goes on to quote examples of actual cases. But first he sets the scene with an explanation of how he arrived at his conclusions after a lifetime in psychiatry. 'I believe that consciousness is a phenomenon in its own right and is not simply the result of brain activity. While it is true that during bodily life, consciousness is closely linked with brain activity and largely dependent upon brain function, there are many observations which support the belief that consciousness survives bodily death and that during life it may, on occasion, operate independently.

'Examples are: near-death experiences, remote viewing, verifiable recollections of previous lives, mediumistic phenomena, the occurrence of unlearned language, and, of course, spirit attachment.' One of his cases quoted involves James, an alcoholic aged 40.

Dr Sanderson explains, 'For many years James had been in a state of psychological invalidism, living alone, unemployed, depressed and subject to periodic alcoholic binges. As a child James had been shy and lacked confidence. After an unhappy childhood at private boarding schools, where he did badly, he got to university to study History of Art, but hated it and dropped out in the first year. He started drinking heavily. For some years, he worked in an art gallery, but was solitary and unhappy.

'Catastrophe hit the family, when Ivor, the favourite son, shot himself after a boozy lunch while out alone on the family's country estate. It was James who discovered the body, while on a nocturnal search. The loss devastated the family, several of whom also sought solace in drinking. James spent the next twelve years in therapy of various sorts: psychoanalysis, hospital admissions, rehabilitation for alcoholism and years on anti-depressants. He went to live alone, in a remote area.

'Fear was an overwhelming problem. James could never bring himself to engage with things, for fear of failure. Some brief relationships with girls ended because of his drinking. Once, in a fit of frustration, he smashed many of his possessions.

'When I saw him, he had not worked for 10 years and lived alone, supported by his family. His only social activity was attendance at Alcoholics Anonymous meetings. James had a long-standing relationship with a young woman who was planning to live with him, but there seemed little prospect of this developing into a fruitful relationship.

'James came reluctantly, following pressure from friends, one of whom had sensed a spirit presence. He impressed me as a charming, graceful and deeply feeling man, with good verbal facility, who was moderately depressed and seriously lacking in confidence. James was open to the notion of spirit attachment. (This makes it is easy). In our second session, with James in a relaxed state, I ask if there are any spirits present. The "Yes" finger moves and the brother, Ivor, signifies his presence.

'Speaking in soft, short utterances, Ivor tells how, following his death, which he denies was intentional but 'a dreadful mistake', he had been aware only of his grieving family and his mother's devastation. He had attached to James since this was easier than attaching to the mother, the person with whom he was most strongly bonded.

Although Ivor is ready to leave James, he cannot do so, since he is being held back by his mother. "She must let me go", he says. I ask Ivor to go to the mother and look in her heart. "She's holding tight", he says. I ask for Ivor's guardian angel to request the mother's guardian angel to explain to her that she has no right to hold on to her son; it is her duty to let go. She does so.

'Before helping Ivor to leave, I ask if there are any other spirits present (in James). Ivor is able to identify the presence of Robert, a gardener who had died from a head injury at work, long before James's family moved to the estate. Robert resented the coming of James's parents ("they destroyed the peace").

'Robert leaves, without difficulty, in the company of his wife, Mavis, who comes for him. He describes a "shaft of light, an opening in the dark." Ivor also goes into the Light, which he describes as "everywhere". He is met by an uncle, who is "beaming".

'Following the release, James feels empty. I call healing spirits to fill the spaces with golden-white light and then to heal the whole subtle energy system - chakras and aura. I conclude by thanking the unseen helpers. I ask if there are any child parts of James that need help. A newborn baby is identified. James is encouraged to take him in his arms. "Safe!" He says. He takes the baby into his heart. "That feels like an integration".

'We have two more sessions at which James is helped to cut ties with his mother. I find him transformed, lively and almost bubbling. Two weeks later he writes, "I seem to have ten times more energy, and yesterday accomplished more than was usual in a week. No crashing out in the afternoons either, and not a suicidal thought in sight. I feel as positive, healthy and happy as I ever have been. I know this has a great deal to do with the work we did together, in particular sorting out the family triangle of Ivor, my mother and myself. She has been considerably improved of late as well".

'Three months later he marries the girl mentioned earlier. In a letter a few days after, he writes, "My mother keeps saying, 'I haven't felt so happy since before Ivor died'. Several months after the marriage, James remains well and happy. He still attends AA several times weekly, although he has not touched alcohol for three years. This is a comparatively simple case.

'Points of particular note are:

1 The dramatic benefit, brought by spirit release, after years of emotional invalidism.

2 Depression and alcohol dependence are two common conditions often associated with   spirit attachment.

3 Attached spirits have frequently experienced violent death.

4 Spirit attachment is often a two-way process.

5 There is a need for healing and other measures following release.'

What a story. Is this Spirit Release business a common practice in psychiatry?

I wouldn't say it was common, but it is widespread. If you Google the subject there are scores of entries. You could debate for ever whether there really are spirits that dominate the human psyche but, the point is, the therapy seems to work and many people with long standing mental and physical issues are often completely cured.

**The human mind will not be confined to any limits -
Johann Wolfgang von Goethe**

15 I THINK I'VE DIED AND GONE TO HEAVEN

We have now learned that the whole universe at its most fundamental level comprises consciousness, and the consciousness that permeates the Universe dwells within each of us. The nexus between the two becomes most apparent to us when we enter an Altered State.

This whole concept of a universal inter-connectedness is exciting and liberating. There is, after all, a meaning to everything. There is a destiny that is unfolding and we are part of it. Each of us is a fundamental component of a Grand Plan. While we retain our free will and must make our own choices, the future we are shaping is a future that is already there only waiting to be made real by our human consciousness.

So how do we attain this altered state? There are many ways like, for instance, meditation, or hypnosis, controlled breathing, chanting, dancing and sleep deprivation. These are the 'natural' ways. The 'unnatural' methods (which I don't recommend as they hand over control to dangerous entities) are narcotics, herbal extracts, alcohol, inhaling solvents and gases, to name but a few. I give a few tips on meditation later in this chapter.

The secret of attaining a meaningful Altered State is a condition of 'unselfconsciousness.' What do I mean by unselfconscious? Think of sleepwalkers, the hypnotised, martial artists, saints and sages, meditators, some children, madmen and drunks. These people have lost their egos and, as a result, appear to have access to a primal, childlike state of Mind which is in touch with the collective unconscious – much like a Zen Buddhist (or a dowser) – and, Hey Presto! You become what people call psychic.

Google 'How do I become psychic?' and you could spend weeks sifting through beguiling offers from mediums, tarot readers, spiritualist circles, mystics, clairvoyants, astrologers, religious gurus and, yes, even psychics. But, as I've already said, I believe the simplest and most straightforward way to become a skilled psychic is through dowsing (an Altered State in itself).

Hypnosis is another way of tuning into the Infinite Mind. Once in a trance the subject can mentally roam far and wide – not just in space but in time as well. You could see it as the hypnotised person entering a different dimension to the rest of us. One of those different dimensions is the realm of Past Lives. And there are many hypnotherapists these days who specialise in taking their clients back – apparently to experience an earlier earthly incarnation. And one of the greatest past life practitioners of them all was hypnotherapist and pioneer in Past Life Exploration, Henry Leo Bolduc, who died in 2011.

He says on his website, 'At the age of fifteen I read the best seller, *The Search for Bridey Murphy,* by Morey Bernstein. At the same time, in high school, we were studying the scientific method. I hoped to apply strict, scientific scrutiny to the book's premise, which was the subject of past lives. The research was successful, and through the decades, I was able to develop various methods, techniques, and tools for people to utilize.'

He then recounts some of the cases he dealt with that subsequently provided material for seminal books on the subject. 'Revelations of death and the post-death experience soon became evident as people spoke of their previous lifetimes and of the death experiences that completed those lifetimes. Some spoke of "staying around" for a few days after the physical body had died. Sometimes, their soul or spirit (or some other non-physical form of energy) stayed to attend their own funeral!

Henry says, 'After the death experience was reported or re-experienced, I usually asked the person about the soul lesson or spiritual review of the past lifetime. It was apparent that even after death, souls continued to study, to learn, to love, and to grow in other dimensions. Everyone can learn to recall deep memories, but only a few can truly learn from the past. Many continue to re-run or to deny experiences rather than to learn from them.'

Henry talks of the benefits of the therapy: 'Past-life exploration contains many bonuses, such as helping people to overcome the fear of death. Many have said that death is a pleasant state, even though the cause of dying might have been gruesome. Death can be thought of as a graduation rather than a punishment - as a continuing adventure, as opposed to oblivion.

'By the grace of God, I have learned that there is a continuity to life - that life is eternal, there is one life with many lifetimes. The harsh things we do to others eventually return as experiences for us to heal. The good we do for others comes back to bless us. What we put into our world eventually returns to us in another lifetime.'

As a Board Certified Regression Therapist, with 45 years of experience in the field, Henry had conducted past-life regression sessions with thousands of people and, as mentioned, wrote several books and hundreds of articles about his work. 'Naive people say jokingly, "Oh, when you talk of past lives, why is everybody Cleopatra or Mark Anthony?"

'But I say from experience that everyone was not a Cleopatra or Mark Anthony. We were street sweepers, murderers, cutthroats, rogues, and whores. We were also priests, priestesses, healers, helpers, nurturing mothers, and providing fathers. We were varied people with varied life experiences, just as we are today. Within this context, only cynics will declare that we were all famous personalities and only egotists will hope so.'

The Mind having a separate and independent existence from the brain is a factor in phenomena like Near-Death and Out-of-Body Experiences. NDEs are states of altered consciousness that can occur in the context of a life-threatening event, such as a heart attack or near drowning. More and more people are becoming acquainted with the topic through a spate of books and films. Audiences were captivated by the 2014 movie *Heaven Is for Real*, about a young boy who told his parents he had visited heaven while he was having emergency surgery. It was based on a book, published in 2010, which sold over 10 million copies.

NDEs were brought even further into the respectable mainstream by two further books written by doctors - *Proof of Heaven*, by Eben Alexander, who tells of a near-death experience he had while in a week-long coma brought on by meningitis, and *To Heaven and Back*, by Mary C Neal, who had her NDE while submerged in a river after a kayaking accident.

I cover the Mind's role in these phenomena in *Dowse Your Way To Psychic Power* so I won't repeat it in detail here. But it is worth introducing a couple of examples to give a flavour of the anomaly which points to the Mind being independent of our bodies.

At the age of 35 Pam Reynolds underwent a rare operation to remove a giant aneurysm in her brain. The procedure involved lowering her temperature to 60 degrees F, her heartbeat and breathing to be stopped, her brain waves flattened, and the blood drained from her head. In everyday terms, her body was being put to death.

The doctor then turned on a surgical saw and began to cut through Pam's skull. Suddenly, Pam felt herself 'pop' outside her body and hover above the operating table. She watched the doctors sawing into her skull and heard what the nurses in the operating room were saying. Meanwhile, every monitor attached to Pam's body registered 'no life' whatsoever.

Then, Pam's consciousness floated out of the operating room and travelled down a tunnel which had a light at the end of it containing her dead relatives and friends, who emanated total love. Pam's NDE ended when her uncle led her back to her body. She says, 'I didn't want to get into it ... It looked terrible, like a train wreck. It looked like what it was: dead.' Then she slipped into it which Pam described as like 'plunging into a pool of ice.'

Barbara Bartolome, 31, also had her experience while on the operating table. '...the next second I was up on the ceiling looking down at the entire room. There was this feeling of a presence that was next to me. It felt like it was God. It felt so loving and so accepting, and so eternal. I literally looked down and said, "Huh, if I'm up here, and my body's down there, then I think I must have just died."'

Barbara began calmly talking to the presence and telling it how much she wanted to go back to her baby daughter and eight-year-old son. Promising to make changes in her life, Barbara was suddenly back. 'I shut my eyes up on the ceiling, and reopened them and found myself looking right into the orthopaedic surgeon's face.'

Of her detachment from her body she says, 'The loss of fear of death was so amazing.' Barbara says she wants people who are facing death to know they don't need to be afraid of it.

She says her purpose now is to spread love, hope and understanding.

Another aspect of the Mind removing itself from its host is encountered in the phenomenon of:

Reincarnation

This is where ordinary people have an overwhelming feeling that they have lived on this earth before. Like, for instance, six-year-old James Leininger who was a normal child except he was obsessed with aircraft and talked about them all the time, even claiming he had been a fighter pilot in a previous life. His parents, Andrea and Bruce, were understandably sceptical. But, gradually, their scepticism evaporated as James began to give convincing details of his exploits.

The parents pieced together that their son had been a 21-year-old US Navy fighter pilot on a mission during the Second World War over the Pacific when was shot down by Japanese artillery. James 'remembered' the pilot's name as James M Huston Jr, the location where he was shot down in Iwo Jima and even the name of the aircraft carrier - Natoma - that he claimed to have taken off from. All the facts checked out. 'It was like, holy mackerel!' Bruce said. 'You could have poured my brains out of my ears. I just couldn't believe it.'

Bruce says he now believes his son had a past life in which he was James Huston. 'He came back because he wasn't finished with something.' The Leiningers wrote a letter to Huston's sister, Anne Barron, about their little boy. And now she believes it as well. 'The child was so convincing in coming up with all the things that there is no way on the world he could know,' she said.

Another reincarnation case was of a three-year-old boy from the Golan Heights, near Syria, who was born with a red birthmark on his head. He claimed this was from being murdered in a past life. Physician Dr Eli Lasch was determined to investigate the story and so took the lad to various locations in Israel until the boy claimed to recognise a village. As they wandered through its streets the boy approached a man and said, 'I used to be your neighbour. We had a fight and you killed me with an axe.'

Then, the boy led Lasch and the accused man to a spot where he claimed his body had been buried. A skeleton was found in the ground with a wound in the skull corresponding to the boy's birthmark. The man eventually confessed to having murdered his neighbour four years earlier.

Hundreds of books have been written, full of case studies of people whose Minds seemed to contain the emotions, experiences and memories of someone completely different –

sometimes of a different sex, religion or ethnic group. Could it be that the consciousness that makes us who we are is really our eternal soul undergoing different earthly incarnations in order to learn valuable lessons along the way? Sounds plausible but how does this fit in with the theory that all time is now?

Another phenomena in which the Mind seems to float freely and travel widely, although remaining with one host, is:

Remote viewing

This is defined as 'the ability to acquire accurate information about a distant or non-local place, person or event without using your physical senses or any other obvious means.' In other words it's being able spontaneously to know something without actually being able to prove how you got the information.

Physicists Russell Targ and Harold Puthoff, parapsychology researchers at Stanford Research Institute are generally credited with coining the term 'remote viewing' to distinguish it from the closely related concept of clairvoyance.

The notion of remote viewing became public knowledge in the 1990s when certain documents relating to the US Government programme called the Stargate Project were released. They revealed experiments designed to determine if there was any potential military application for psychic phenomena. One of these experiments was remote viewing.

The concept was explored by psychic researcher Ingo Swann, who worked in controlled laboratory settings with scientists for over 20 years. In one of his most extraordinary experiments in 1973 he 'visited' the planet Jupiter in a joint 'psychic probe' shared by fellow sensitive Harold Sherman. Swann's drawings made during the experiment showed a 'ring' of tiny asteroids around the planet which scientists at the time said did not exist but which were later – in 1979 - scientifically confirmed.

These days there are many seductive courses on the internet promising to teach us how to detach our Mind and send it out to bring back information. A few people will have the discipline to achieve some success in this. But most won't because it takes up too much time and effort and only a handful have the natural gift for it. However, this doesn't negate the achievements of some who have produced results impossible to explain with conventional science.

And a different skill which is equally mysterious and jaw-dropping is one specific aspect of divining which defies rational belief. It's called Map Dowsing, where the dowser with a pendulum hovers over a map and, somehow, manages to connect, virtually, with the real-life location.

The skill has wide variety of applications: from finding your lost car keys to locating an oil well or a diamond mine. The map does not even have to be perfect or accurately drawn to scale. It can be a simple sketch on a piece of paper. For instance, a rough plan of a house is often good enough to allow a dowser specialising in Geopathic Stress to detect and eliminate detrimental energies within a person's home, sometimes located thousands of miles away.

UK dowser Peter Taylor is contracted by oil companies to locate profitable fields all over the world *while sitting at home using a geological map.* A typical example, which could not have been more far-flung, was the challenge of identifying an oil field in Central Australia.

Said Peter, 'The company's geologist had come up with the same results that I had. The difference being, his geologist was on site in Australia, and I had map dowsed here in the United Kingdom.'

Moving with the times Peter now uses Google Earth to locate mineral deposits, including gold and diamonds, anywhere around the world. He says, 'This method of remote map surveying/dowsing is far more accurate than the ordnance survey maps I had to rely on in the past.' So, how can a human Mind connect with a physical location thousands of miles away, just by focusing on an image? No-one knows.

199

Map dowsing is used extensively in Russia, particularly for military targets. The Russians are not so dismissive of the counter-intuitive aspects of the practice – they just do it.

One of the most dramatic examples of Map Dowsing is attributed to legendary dowser and inventor of the world's most complex dowsing tool, Verne Cameron (1896-1970).

In 1959, during the Cold War, he was written to by US Vice Admiral Maurice E Curtis, who clearly had in mind the possibility of gaining a military advantage over the country's adversaries. In his letter, dated 18 March, Admiral Curtis said, 'I am advised you believe you may be able to tell the location of all submarines in the world's waters – and their nationalities – by a technique which is called "Map Dowsing."'

The Admiral then suggested Cameron demonstrate his prowess 'at a place of your choice on the West Coast.' Cameron accepted the challenge with alacrity and proceeded to shock his military audience by identifying the whereabouts of every single US submarine on a world map. He then went on to do the same with the Soviet submarine fleet. He was subsequently sent home by tight-lipped officials and only found out belatedly that his passport had been rendered invalid and he had been designated a security risk and therefore banned from leaving the country!

By the way, the dowsing tool that he invented is called the Aurameter, a five-in-one dowsing rod which can be used as a compass, pendulum, pointer, wand and counting mechanism. It is considered by professional dowsers to be one of the most sensitive instruments on the market.

Another but equally dramatic instance of Map Dowsing changed one woman's life:

In 1991, when her daughter's rare, hand-carved harp was stolen, Associate Professor Elizabeth Lloyd Mayer, clinical supervisor at the University of California, Berkeley's Psychology Clinic, did something extraordinary for a dyed-in-the-wool scientific thinker. After the police failed to turn up any leads, a friend suggested she call a dowser, who specialised in finding lost objects. With nothing to lose - and almost as a joke - Dr Mayer agreed.

Within two days, and without leaving his Arkansas home 1500 miles away, the dowser located the exact California street coordinates where the harp was found. What followed turned Dr Mayer's familiar world of science and rational thinking upside down. Deeply shaken, yet driven to understand what had happened, Mayer began a fourteen-year journey of discovery which ended in her writing her bestseller *Extraordinary Knowing* that explores what science has to say about this episode and countless other 'inexplicable' phenomena.

From Sigmund Freud's writings on telepathy to secret CIA experiments on remote viewing, from leading-edge neuroscience to the strange world of quantum physics, Dr Mayer researched a wealth of credible and fascinating information about the psychic world where the Mind seems to trump the laws of nature.

Plenty of material here to quiz you on. For a start let's talk more about so-called past lives and reincarnation. In giving examples you've conveniently missed out the weight of evidence against either. There are numerous debunkings of both based on FACT. People in altered states seem to give convincing accounts of their lives until someone checks out the names, dates, and locations and finds they don't, and never have, existed.

I agree. However, often details like period dress, customs, vernacular, dialect and other local colour do check out. And it's the kind of information not to be found in books, which rules out the regressed person just dredging up from their subconscious things they've read about or seen in films. This seems to suggest that the experience is genuine.

If that is the case, how do you explain that, nearly always, proof is impossible to find?

By now you should be able to come up with your own ideas. For instance, if you go along with the Many Worlds Theory you could extrapolate that the Mind re-visited just ONE time-line out of billions available. So while the past life traveller is accurately describing their world, the sceptic is investigating a slightly different one where some details are tantalisingly similar but others don't match.

Huh! So it's a stand-off – you can't prove your theory to me and I can't convince you.

I don't claim to have the answers. All I am trying to do is get my reader to appreciate the miracle of the human Mind and all the possibilities it offers.

I guess the same principle applies to Near-Death Experiences... 'Pam's consciousness floated out of the operating theatre...' Indeed! There are scientific explanations for these anomalies, like the brain is able to absorb information around it, even though it is medically flat-lining. Or the brain compensates for its state by creating hallucinations. But you seem to prefer the woo-woo version of events.

I have to respect the opinions of people with vast experience in their field. For instance Dr Pim van Lommel, a Dutch cardiologist who began to be intrigued by stories from patients whose hearts had stopped, and then went on to become a recognised world authority on near-death experiences. He says, 'After many years of research it has become clear to me, beyond a reasonable doubt, that there is a continuity of consciousness after the death of our physical body.'

Explaining his theory more fully he says, 'When the brain is turned off, like the tv set or radio, the waves of our consciousness remain. Death is only the end of our physical body. In other words, we have a body but we ARE consciousness. It is hard to avoid the conclusion that our essential consciousness existed before our birth and will exist after we die. It has no beginning and no end.' Incidentally, Dr van Lommel covers this topic in detail in his book *Consciousness Beyond Life*.

If our consciousness just detaches and floats off when we die, could this explain things like possession because the principle is very similar? With reincarnation the Mind of someone previously alive seems to drop into another body being born, so why can't a Mind drop into someone who is living a normal, earthly life?

If you accept the idea that 'we' are not our bodies but a consciousness – our spirit if you like – then it is all too logical that this consciousness, once released from its earthly bonds, can invade a living body and squat rather like a cuckoo in the nest.

And that would be possession?

Yes.

Returning back to earth, it seems I can't utilise the full potential of my Mind unless I'm in some kind of altered state. And you say one of the ways of getting into this state is to meditate. Is there a fairly simple way for a busy person to do this?

Yes. The idea of meditation is to shut out the 'chattering monkey' of thoughts going on in your head. Not as easy as it sounds. So, the first thing to do is enter the whole experience without any high expectations. Don't ask too much of yourself. And keep is simple.

1 As a beginner set a time limit – say 15 minutes.

2 Find a peaceful place to sit where you won't be disturbed.

3 Sit in a chair with your feet on the floor and your hands lightly clasped in your lap, or one hand on each knee.

Just make sure you are stable and in a position you can stay in for a while.

4 Close your eyes and take a deep breath, hold it for a couple of seconds and let it out.   Do this three times. This will relax your body. Then breathe normally, but be aware of your breath   as it goes in and out.

5 Inevitably, your attention will wander. Just bring it back and concentrate on minutely   examining the inside of your eyelids. At first you will just see swirls and lines. As you continue to concentrate, however, pictures will start to form. Don't try to make sense of   them. Simply watch with detachment.

6 Don't obsess over the content of the images or try to analyse them. This process is your   gateway   to   the unconscious - but it will take practice to develop that portal. Meantime,   come back whenever feels right.

7 When you're ready, open your eyes and take a moment to notice the environment   around you. Note how your body feels and be aware of your thoughts and emotions.

8 Feel good about yourself and make a date to repeat the exercise. Practice makes perfect. That portal awaits.

EPILOGUE

There is a story that the ancients came to earth, bringing with them the secrets of eternity. But they worried about how to hide these great secrets until humankind was spiritually ready to appreciate and appropriately use them.

One lamented, 'If we hide them on land, people will conquer the land and discover them.' Another commented, 'If we hide them in the sea, humans will reach the very bottom and uncover them.' A third observed, 'If we hide them in space, men and women will one day conquer even that.' They pondered. Then the wisest said, 'Let us hide these secrets in the last place they will think to look - in their own minds.'

And this proved to be the perfect hiding place.

FINAL THOUGHTS (WELL ALMOST)

A lot of stuff we've covered can be a bit Mind-swamping so here's a quick-fire recap of the main points:

Your Mind has a power beyond belief and you, in partnership with the Infinite Mind, are co-creating the world we live in – past, present and future

But, beware, sameness and tedium is the enemy of Mind Power and can stilt the magic – so occasionally change the pattern of your life

The Universe requires, demands and expects participation

The Infinite Mind provides you with the tools to do the job

Our thoughts are energy and energy cannot be destroyed so thoughts – good or evil - reverberate for ever

Intent manifests your objective

Belief can change reality. Belief can heal. Belief can kill

All the cells in our bodies contain our consciousness, like a hologram

The Observer (you) Creates Reality

Mind is NOT the brain and it can float freely, detached from its host

We live in an invisible soup of energies – natural and man-made – which affect our physical, emotional and mental beings all the time

Unseen energies have power – they can kill

Mind can create detrimental energies affecting locations, homes and workplaces. But Mind also has the power to transmute negative energies into positive. It can clear the soup!

Mind can reach back into the past and change it – and Stephen Hawking agrees

Consciousness (Mind) creates space and time

Consciousness suffuses the Universe

Conscious intent can be transferred to objects, including water

Humble though we may feel, with the help of the Infinite Mind we can change anything

Our Mind has a mind of its own and can go its own way

Our unconscious Mind carries out 95% of our daily lives

The sickness reaches out for the cure

Nobody understands Quantum Mechanics

When we make a choice we 'collapse the wave function' and create a new reality

When we make a choice we create a new Universe (according to the Many Worlds Theory)

Dowsing plugs our intuition into the Universal Consciousness

And so does Kinesiology (muscle-testing)

The human Mind is like a computer terminal plugged into a giant database – according to Prof David Hawkins

Everything in the Universe is connected

Colours have their own wavelength and can heal because they interact with our energy bodies

Hypnosis is one way of focusing the power of the Mind

Meditation is another

Our Minds can 'plug in' to the Information Field 'out there'

And become a genius

Everything around us has a form of intelligence – even your fridge!

Do not play with a Ouija Board – it's like opening your front door and shouting 'Anyone want to come in?'

Yes, those energies that surround us include not-so-friendly discarnate spirits who would love to share your body

If you want to connect with the Infinite Mind, lose your ego

There is a heaven – at least Near-death experiencers say there is

Our Minds are independent from our brains and can roam backwards and forwards in time and space

Our Minds are immortal

If you fancy a longer ponder you might like to think about this:

Time as a linear process is an illusion. Time is now - past, present and future is NOW. Imagine being in a helicopter and time is a stream winding all the way from the left hand side of your vision to disappear off to the right. Jesus is being born over to the left and a bit nearer is the Battle of Hastings and a bit nearer still is the World Wars of the 20th Century. Immediately below is Today and winding off to the right is the future. But you can see it all at a glance in the NOW.

The entire universe is made up of trillions of jiggling frequencies that fill all matter and the 'empty' space in between…the particles that make up atoms, that make up matter, are jumping in and out of existence and, according to Quantum Theory, can be in two places at the same time.

The Mind is a powerful instrument whose waves, allied to strong emotion, cause disturbances in this jiggling fabric and can reach back into the 'past' and forward into the 'future' because time is actually NOW.

Because we are connected with everything, influences can work both ways and our Minds can be penetrated by ideas floating about in the Cosmos. This is how geniuses get their inspiration.

Many of the weirdnesses of quantum mechanics would be solved by the 'Many Worlds' theory whereby every conscious decision 'creates' our reality and sets up 'shadow' realities in other universes where millions of other versions of ourselves pursue different lives. Thus we all have eternal life as, while this dimension's body may die, our other selves continue in other universes.

Also, we may see our daily lives as being stuck in a groove akin to those on an old-fashioned vinyl record. Occasionally we may 'jump' out of the groove and find ourselves in the groove next door where everything appears normal except for strange, small differences.

Dr Nikolai A Kozyrev has a theory that 'The Field' is time and that it varies in 'density' to create differing realities. Einstein might have agreed as he believed space is time and time is space.

APPENDIX 1

The Double-Slit Experiment

One of the most fundamental pieces of research that has thrown die-hard classical scientists into disarray is the celebrated Double-Slit Experiment. Hold onto your hats because the implications of this experiment led to my Eureka! moment. The Double-Slit Experiment is where light is shone at a screen with two parallel slits cut in it. This causes an outline of light and dark strips to be formed on another screen behind. These strips of light and dark are called an interference pattern, caused by light spreading out from the two slits in a series of overlapping waves.

However, when photons - single particles of light (think of little marbles) are fired at the slits there should be no pattern as there are no waves to 'interfere' with each other. But, inexplicably, there is still an interference pattern reflected on the wall. How can this be when there are no waves to overlap? Experimenters concluded that single photons seemed to be able to go through two slits at the same time. This meant that each particle has a ghostly twin in another universe mimicking its every move.

Even more incredibly, it also seems as if the photons can read the experimenters' Minds because, as each single photon is fired, the interference effect builds up on the screen according to a pattern anticipated by the human watchers! Also, scientists found that the particles seemed to know that they were being watched and adjusted their behaviour accordingly. When physicists tested for the presence of particles they got particles; when they tested for light waves, they got waves. It seems that the test itself tried to oblige the humans involved by determining a result they desired, which is utterly alien to classical physics.

I know this seems crazy, but stay with it because things get even weirder.

Confirming that there seems to be an apparent intelligence at work, the particles become overtly coy when the experiment is taken on a stage. When the experimenters set up a detector to measure which slit each particle goes through, the photons refused to behave like waves and remained as particles creating one spot on the screen as one might expect. As soon as the detector is switched off, the particles resume behaving like waves, creating an interference pattern!

One conclusion that could be drawn is that the Mind of man creates reality. But there is another deduction even more fundamental.

215

According to American physicist Richard Feynman, the unexplained behaviour of photons and electrons applies to all sub-atomic particles and the Double-Slit Experiment goes to the core of the quantum mystery (there are excellent visual explanations of the Double-Slit Experiment on YouTube).

A further refinement of the experiment takes us into the realms of the profound and provides the basis for answers to metaphysical questions like What is life for? Why are we here? If there is a God why does he allow suffering? This refinement of the experiment is known as Delayed Choice. Here, a detector is set up between the two screens to monitor the particular route a particle is taking AFTER it has passed through the slits but BEFORE it hits the screen. Remember, if the particle 'thinks' it is being monitored it remains a photon resulting in a blob of light on the screen. However, if it is not being monitored it is quite happy to behave like a wave and go through two slits at the same time.

By setting up the monitor between the screens, theoretically it will be too late for the particle to decide whether to be a photon or a wave, as it will already have made the choice and gone through the slit. Amazingly though, when the monitor is switched on the particle remains a particle and when switched off the particle behaves like a wave and creates a typical interference pattern. This means that the photon already knows what mode the monitor will be in BEFORE it passes through the slit. How? Does it read the experimenters' Minds? Can it tell the future? (Personally, I believe for the wave function to collapse it only requires the observer to be CAPABLE of knowing which slit the photon went through – not actually knowing).

These experiments were conducted independently of each other by the University of Maryland in the US and the University of Munich in Germany.

If you extrapolate these results to a cosmic scale, and use two beams of diffracted light from a star millions of light years away, the particles and waves would behave in the same way by appearing on your screen as blobs of light or an interference pattern, depending on whether your monitor was switched on or off. Which means that, as the light from the star has taken millions of years to arrive on earth, it must have 'known' when it first began its journey that it was going to be monitored. Before the human species had even begun to evolve. How? Does this support the argument of Predestination? That everything is pre-ordained by a Creator for whom we are vital partners?

So the quantum universe has thrown up paradoxes and weirdnesses that rival anything the world of the paranormal can manage. Some scientists try to explain it by suggesting that there could be an infinite number of realities which exist alongside our own. Every choice of life is made within these other realities and our lives progress according to our choices, which creates our reality. So, you might marry, have children and divorce in this life whereas in the Universe next door you might remain single and in the parallel world next to that you might die as a child. The Universe is a seething mass of probabilities and only human consciousness can 'conjure' any of those probabilities into reality. I hope you are now convinced just why you are so important – the Universe needs you!

And, part of our consciousness that exists outside ourselves (the Mind) pursues at a quantum level the choices we did not make, giving part of us an existence in all the other parallel worlds in which the infinite number of options are being played out. Whether you go along with this theory or not, it is another pointer to our Minds and thoughts having powerful effects on the world (and worlds) about us.

That –is –so –exciting!

APPENDIX 2

Don't succumb to the 'little me' syndrome

What can an ordinary person like you or me do about all that's going wrong in the world? If we believe half of what we've read in this book, the answer is: more than we could know. First, let's take an actual example of something containing bad energy. And, don't forget, bad energy can be anything that causes a detrimental effect to human or any sentient life. This can range from a simple cursed object like a wedding ring to a neighbourhood, community or country where evil seems to be triumphing (think the rise of Nazism in the 1930s or the Islamic State, or what's going on in Syria today).

First get yourself into a restful state of mind; some might call this meditation but, in reality, it's any condition in which the mind is relaxed. Then, visualise your own version of what those bad energies might look like. This might simply be black waves of radiating energy, or you could imagine a spiteful face and an angry, pointing finger, or maybe hordes of evil, rampaging beings creating havoc. It doesn't matter, so long as you have a vivid image in your Mind.

Gradually, bring the 'target' (cursed ring, problem school, neighbourhood etc), complete with your own unique image of how the detrimental energies are affecting it, into mind and start focusing. Get the objective firmly in your sights, as if it's a scene playing out on a brightly lit stage, to the exclusion of everything else. Your focus of attention should be unambiguous – link strongly to the person, thing or place.

Then, remembering you are working in partnership with the Infinite Mind, with which you are quantum-ly entangled (don't forget you are a co-creator with it) start to transmute the negative energies into beneficial ones. Again, you vividly visualise the 'baddies' being overcome by forces of good and you radiate unconditional love to fill the hole left. However you picture it, it will work because it is your own unique creation.

The ring is washed clean under a sparkling waterfall, the neighbourhood's riots are quelled and the participants smile and start to embrace one another …you get the idea. I find it useful to put this exercise into words like:

'I remove all detrimental energies from this (object/school/prison/community/country) and replace them with beneficial energies to bring balance, harmony, health and healing to its complete being – physical, emotional, mental and spiritual.' What you have done is give a clear set of instructions to your 'partner,' the Infinite Mind. Then get out of the way and let the Infinite Mind do its work. Those of a religious bent might sum this up as 'Let Go and Let God.'

This process selects the appropriate quantum possibility out of the billions available, and the wave function collapses. What you have just done, in terms of Quantum Physics, is select a different outcome from the list of infinite possibilities and create a new reality. Your Mind has performed a modern miracle.

APPENDIX 3

More nuggets to ponder (I know, this is really testing your patience – sorry)

All controversial experiments (which often can't be repeated in a laboratory) work because of the inventor/creator's INTENT and BELIEF, plus the morphic field built up around its location, plus the expectation of the audience/recipients. Thus it's the consciousness of the creator which is the essential ingredient, not the methodology – eg in homeopathy, it's the practitioner's INTENT that creates the healing, not the tincture.

The most important factor in healing a sick person, house or environment is to accept the possibility and the most important part of healing is our intention for it to occur.

The Infinite Mind respects intercession.

The more you analyse it the less it works (analysing depletes intent). Don't fall into the trap of 'paralysis by analysis.'

We must live how we want to change the world – create harmony within ourselves (if you want to change the world, first change yourself). It's the state we are in, not something we do, that changes the Universe. Thus you can sit at home sending harmonious thoughts to your neighbourhood, which will do more good than a battalion of riot police.

Bruce Lipton proved that stem cells in a Petri dish, left in a sick environment, got sick and vice versa. 'We are Petri Dishes enclosed in skin. If we are left in a sick environment we get sick. Disease is not genetic – it comes from the environment.'

All the cells in our bodies are affected by our thought processes.

To be successful in your endeavours you must live your life in a sublime spirit of confidence and determination – disregard appearances, conditions, in fact all evidence of your senses that deny the fulfilment of your aims. Ignore the present state and assume the intent fulfilled. BELIEVE.

The act of dowsing sends the intent. In dowsing, what you are seeking is also seeking you!

Focused intention crosses all boundaries of time and space.

223

The reason Radionics works is that the procedure creates a conviction in the practitioner's Mind that something concrete is being done and is <u>continuing to be done</u> (the dials are set and the rate selected and the process is launched).

INTENT is powerful – but use gentle wishing rather than intense willing or striving.

Intention affects physical reality.

Personal, sustained, specific intention influences substances, people and events – William   Tiller.

Objects can absorb human thought and hold them for hundreds of years.

Never finish a negative statement; reverse it and wonders will happen in your life. And if   you   can't   say something nice about a person, don't say anything at all.

A new step in personal development is often accompanied by a feeling of fatigue.

In the realm of all possibilities, everything already exists.

Be grateful – gratitude drives out fear and tunes you into the Universe.

Energy is liberated matter – matter is energy in bondage.

DOWSING INFO

Don't think about it – just do it.

The pendulum will also react to ideas – 'Shall I write a book?'

To become a successful dowser we must drive hard to improve – no matter what it takes.

Doubt short-circuits the dowsing connection.

Dowsing programmes your intent.

Treat everything as if it has its own consciousness and dialogue with that consciousness.

Detrimental energies in your home can come from a previous resident, *reflecting them as they are today.*

When dowsing (as in life), cultivate an attitude of gratitude.

APPENDIX 4

A practical healing protocol - using Subtle Energy Therapy

For those readers who are healers, or those who may want to be healers, here's a simple modality that works.

Start with an introductory chat building a 'bridge to believability,' explaining that the client is taking what he/she needs from you rather than you giving the client what they need. This puts the onus on the client who may be self-sabotaging.

Define the issue – back pain, illness, phobia (if necessary dowse for this? – remember, the act of dowsing opens a portal to channeling information from other dimensions).

The client must sincerely accept the process – self sabotage will block the flow of energies – muscle test for this (does s/he really WANT help?).

The client's Higher Self knows that the answer to his/her problems lies within the Universal Life Force and you, the healer, connects both up. The client MUST take continuing ownership of the exercise.

As in Dissociative Identity Disorder and quantum's creating a new reality, the aim is to create a different person – one without the health issue.

1   Need (never forget, the need has found you, you haven't found the need).

2 Knowledge of need creates quantum entanglement (beware – too much acknowledgement reinforces the reality and makes it more self aware).

3 Dowse the cause of the issue – and don't forget it could possibly be spirit possession – all illness has a spirit.

4 Send your intent to heal, inviting a new possibility, which gets the Universal Life Force flowing, which collapses the wave function and alters reality. This activates and promotes the needing entity's ability to heal itself. THE NEED TAKES HEALING FROM YOU, YOU DON'T GIVE IT.

5 Declare your verdict with confidence (You think this is a risk but your perception of your limitations is just an illusion: the healing is already in existence – your intervention creates its reality.

6 Disconnect. You have introduced the 'Life Force' to the need – now step back and BE DETACHED FROM THE OUTCOME (very important) and act as though the objective

has already been achieved. And have an attitude of gratitude that a new reality has been created.

7 Give the client a symbol to remind them of the daily presence in their lives of the Universal Life Force – perhaps give them the radionics 'rate'? Or a healing crystal?

8 The healing ALWAYS works for the ultimate good of those who acknowledge receiving the flow of the Universal Life Force (although the outcome may not be what they expect).

Important things for you, the healer, to remember:

1 You are sharing healing energy (not doing healing on someone). This keeps the ego at bay. One of the greatest keys to success is to stay out of your own way

2 Healer & healee are coming together each to create a personal experience for themselves. This avoids the 'trying to…' attitude.

3 The healer is a channel for the Universal Life Force Energy to flow through. The more you can receive and BE the energy, as opposed to trying to make it work, the more powerful it will be. You need to ALLOW the energy to flow, not cause it to happen.

4 No judgements – judgements block the flow.

5 Feel CONNECTED to the healee...we are both energy from the same ocean of energy. The healing is flowing for US.

6 Unconditional love sees the person not the behaviour. Unconditional love IS healing so find it within yourself where it already exists.

7 Be continuously grateful to the Creator for the privilege of performing healing work.

8 This whole process above has 'raised the vibrations' enabling the ULF to flow.

Note: All healing modalities have one thing in common – they all collapse the wave function. Important: The human intent acts as a transformer and receives cosmic energy in its raw state and converts it to he exact frequency required by the need.

Essential ingredients for successful healing: Need, Belief (irrational optimism), Directed Intent (to move energy), Focus, Detachment (of the ego), Sincerity.

A WORD FROM THE AUTHOR

If you have enjoyed this book please consider writing a review on the Amazon site. And if you believe the book is worth sharing, please take a few seconds to let your friends know about it.

A bit about myself

My interest in the paranormal began with a car crash. I was driving back to my home in Sussex having just bought my first, brand-new Triumph Spitfire convertible. As I tootled along with the top down I decided to test its performance and pressed down on the accelerator. Before I knew it I had hit 60mph on a suburban dual carriageway.

Suddenly a car hurtled, backwards, out of a driveway right into my path. I wrenched on the steering wheel but, due to my inexperience with this particular car, I over-corrected and found myself crashing across the central reservation and spinning into heavy traffic coming from the other direction. I

remember thinking to myself, 'What a stupid way to die...'
Then, all noise seemed to cease and I found 'myself' floating
above that young man in the driving seat watching him fighting
for control as if I was viewing a film. The floating 'I' was
utterly detached and filled with compassion for 'him' (not
'me') and thinking, 'how sad.'

Then, abruptly, I was back in my body again and the air was
filled with the crashing and grinding of metal as I eventually
came to a stop against someone's garden wall. Calmly, I
switched off the engine and got out of the wreckage. I hadn't
even been scratched! But that out-of-body episode changed
my life as I realised there is a part of every human being that is
eternal, can float freely and retain some kind of intelligence.

Thus began a lifetime researching what you might call The
Unexplained - the mystical, occult, paranormal, esoteric,
mysterious and Things That Go Bump in the Night. And the
more I studied the more I realised that access to supernatural
powers is not confined to the favoured few but is open to us all.
What gives us access to these powers is our Minds.
Confirmation of this conclusion came through my interest in
dowsing, which I was astonished to find retrained my mind to
create a portal to other dimensions.

And I realised anyone can do it. I cover all this in more detail
in *Dowse Your Way To Psychic Power*. Meanwhile, my other

book *In Tune With The Infinite Mind* is a good introduction to the whole subject of the power of human consciousness.

With unprecedented changes happening to the Planet and to Humanity there has never been a greater need for positive minds to assert themselves.

If you would like to get in touch please feel free to message me on Facebook.

BIBLIOGRAPHY

PMH Atwater *Future Memory*, Hampton Roads Publishing 1999

Cynthia Sue Larson *Reality Shifts: When Consciousness Changes the Physical World,* Create Space Publishing 2011

Dean Radin *Entangled Minds: Extrasensory Experiences in a Quantum Reality,* Simon & Schuster 2006

Elizabeth Mayer *Extraordinary Knowing*, Bantam Dell Publishing Group 2008

George Applegate *The Complete Guide to Dowsing*, Vega Books 2002

Anthony Talmage *Dowse Your Way To Psychic Power*, Amazon 2015

Anthony Talmage *In Tune With The Infinite Mind,* Create Space 2017

T C Lethbridge *The Power of the Pendulum,* Routledge & Paul 1976

Adrian Incledon Webber *Heal Your Home*, Dowsing Spirits 2013

Kathy Forti *Fractals of God*, Rinnovo Press 2014

ANTHONY TALMAGE

Hans Andeweg *In Resonance With Nature*, Floris Books 2009

Hilary Evans *SLIders – the Enigma of Street Light Interference,* Anomalist Books 2010

Richard Gerber *Vibrational Medicine for the 21st Century,* London, Piatkus 2000

Caryle Hirshberg and Marc Ian Barasch *Remarkable Recovery*, Remarkable Recovery Books 2014

AK Bhattacharya *Teletherapy* 1977

Darius Dinshah *Let There Be Light*, Dinshah Health Society 2001

Bill Bengston *The Energy Cure*, Sounds True 2010

Pim van Lommel *Consciousness Beyond Life*, HarperOne; Reprint edition 2011

Anadi Martel *Light Therapies – A Complete Guide to the Healing Power of Light,* Healing Arts 2018

Edith Fiore *The Unquiet Dead: A Psychologist Treats Spirit Possession,* New York: Ballantine Books 1987

Eben Alexander *Proof of Heaven*, Piatkus; Reprint edition 2012

Mary C Neal *To Heaven and Back*, Authentic Media 2012

Archibald Lawrie *The Psychic Investigator's Handbook,* AuthorHouse UK 2003

William Tiller *Science and Human Transformation*, Pavior Publishing 1997

Carl Wickland *Thirty Years Among the Dead,* National Psychological Institute 1924. This is the definitive, classic work laying the foundations for all future investigations into the nature of earthbound spirits.

William J Baldwin *Healing Lost Souls: Releasing Unwanted Spirits from Your Energy Body,* Charlottesville, VA: Hampton Roads Publishing 2003

Hazel Courteney *Divine Intervention,* Amazon 2011

Rupert Sheldrake *A New Science of Life,* Park Street Press 1995

Rupert Sheldrake *The Presence Of The Past*, Icon Books Ltd 2011

Rupert Sheldrake *Science Set Free*, Deepak Chopra 2013

Danah Zohar *The Quantum Self,* Harper Collins 1991

Kathe Bachler *Earth Radiations,* John Living 2007

Cleve Backster *Primary Perception: Biocommunications with Plants,* White Rose Press, illustrated edition 2003

ANTHONY TALMAGE

Alexandra David-Neel *Magic and Mystery in Tibet,*
University Books 1965

Dr Masaru Emoto *Messages from Water,* Hay House UK
2010

Printed in Great Britain
by Amazon

64474107R00140